# Paul Elvstrøm explains

# Racing Rules of Sailing

## 2001 - 2004 rules

**Edited by Søren Krause**

ADLARD COLES NAUTICAL
London

# FAST FIND DIAGRAM TO PART 2 RULES 'WHEN BOATS MEET'

**Black numbers are the Rule numbers**
**Red numbers refer to the Explanatory Section**

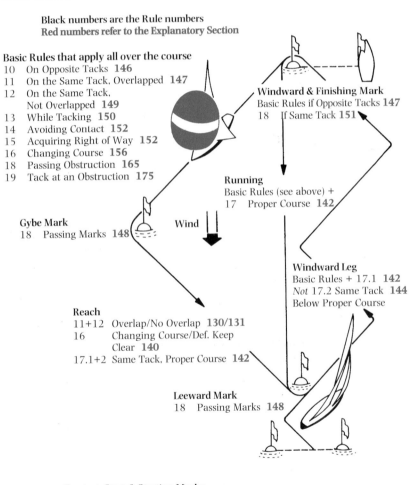

**Basic Rules that apply all over the course**

| | | |
|---|---|---|
| 10 | On Opposite Tacks | **146** |
| 11 | On the Same Tack, Overlapped | **147** |
| 12 | On the Same Tack, Not Overlapped | **149** |
| 13 | While Tacking | **150** |
| 14 | Avoiding Contact | **152** |
| 15 | Acquiring Right of Way | **152** |
| 16 | Changing Course | **156** |
| 18 | Passing Obstruction | **165** |
| 19 | Tack at an Obstruction | **175** |

**Windward & Finishing Mark**
Basic Rules if Opposite Tacks **147**
18    If Same Tack **151**

**Running**
Basic Rules (see above) +
17    Proper Course **142**

**Gybe Mark**
18    Passing Marks **148**

Wind

**Windward Leg**
Basic Rules + 17.1 **142**
*Not* 17.2 Same Tack **144**
Below Proper Course

**Reach**
11+12    Overlap/No Overlap **130/131**
16        Changing Course/Def. Keep Clear **140**
17.1+2 Same Tack, Proper Course **142**

**Leeward Mark**
18    Passing Marks **148**

**Prestart, Start & Starting Marks**
Basic Rules (see above)
*Not* 18! at a Starting Mark **146**
*Not* 17! Same Tack, Proper Course before the Starting Signal **133**

# CONTENTS

Foreword                                                    4

Introduction                                                5

How to get the best use out of this book                    6

Summary of changes in the 2001 – 2004 rules                 7

Brief notes of guidance for making a protest               10

**ISAF RACING RULES SECTION**
(black headband)

Contents of ISAF Rules                                     13

Official text of the ISAF Rules                            15

Official text of the ISAF Appendices                       50

**EXPLANATORY SECTION**
(Red headband)

Explanatory notes with bird's-eye-view
drawings                                                  137

**ISAF INTERPRETATIONS SECTION**
(Red hatched headband)

Summary of cases in the order of the rules                200

Race Signals                                              223

*Rules are cross-referenced to the
Explanations and Interpretations by RED
numbers in the margins*

# FOREWORD

Every four years after the Olympic Games the Racing Rules of Sailing are reviewed. In November 1996 the Rules were revised thoroughly but they are still quite difficult to understand and may be ambiguous in some situations. To help clarify them and ensure uniform interpretation and understanding of their meaning, the ISAF publishes a number of official 'interpretations'.

*Paul Elvstrøm explains the Yacht Racing Rules* provides a ready-reference to the Rules, giving relevant interpretations together with explanatory notes and drawings in a handy pocket-sized book. Its aim is to help officials and competitors alike to learn the rules easily, to understand them, and to apply them correctly. It also enables protests and disputes to be resolved fairly.

*Paul Elvstrøm explains* is therefore an invaluable handbook, providing a concise guide to the Racing Rules of Sailing for everyone involved in racing.

Göran Petersson
Vice President of ISAF
Former Chairman of the
Racing Rules Committee

# INTRODUCTION

The main object of *Paul Elvstrøm explains the Racing Rules of Sailing* is to provide a handy and easily-read guide for all of us to understand and interpret the rules identically.

In 1997 the Racing Rules were entirely rewritten in a shorter and more logical form, using a more modern and easily-read language but they are probably still among the most complicated of any sport. There is a constant flow of new interpretations, clarifications and changes to the rules. The use of the same rules also in match racing has greatly accelerated this process, and introduced a more aggressive use of the rules as a weapon against competitors. The best way to avoid problems is still to sail against others in the same way that we wish to be sailed against. This unwritten rule is the best way of preserving friendships and encouraging participation in sailboat racing.

It is great to win in yacht racing, but only if the other competitors join in the pleasure.

I am happy that Søren, besides being an active racing sailor and a busy international judge/umpire, again has found the time to edit this edition which incorporates the new 2001–2004 Rules.

Paul Elvstrøm

# HOW TO GET THE BEST USE OUT OF THIS BOOK

The book is divided into three sections.

1 ▮ *The Racing Rules of Sailing* as published by the ISAF.

2 ▮ A simple *Explanation* of the various situations that can arise under each rule, supported by bird's-eye-view line drawings.

3 ◺ A precis of most of the *Interpretations of the ISAF Rules*, some with bird's-eye-view line drawings.

Following an incident, look up the appropriate Rule in the BLACK section. This is a facsimile of the ISAF Rules. If you don't know the rule number, you might get help from the Fast Find diagram, page 2, for the 'when boats meet' rules, or in the Rules contents page 13 for the rest of the rules.

In the margin opposite the rule will be cross reference page numbers printed in RED which refers you to the *Explanatory* section with RED headbands. From here a new RED number will take you to the relevant *Interpretation* section with RED HATCHED headbands.

The *Explanatory* section is what it says – an explanation of the rule or rules involved, with line drawings to illustrate the points. In the line drawings, the red boat is either wrong, potentially wrong or in the worst position. This way of thinking, always being aware of who is wrong or RED, has proved very useful when racing, especially in match racing, where it is essential to both competitors and umpires to know who is at fault, even before the incident arises.

To support these explanations, many of the Appeals to the ISAF Rules are summed up in the *Interpretation* section with the RED HATCHED headbands. These form a Case Law for the Racing Rules of Sailing and are an invaluable cross reference. It is recommended that both the serious competitor and also the keen student of the Rules obtains a copy of the full text of the ISAF Interpretations.

I would like to thank the ISAF, especially the members of the Racing Rules Committee, for their help and co-operation in producing this book.

Søren Krause
January 2001

# SUMMARY OF CHANGES IN THE 2001–2004 RULES

In the 1997–2000 edition of the Racing Rules of Sailing, the rules were totally revised. The New Simplified Rules have worked well but, as expected, loopholes and unforeseen consequences have appeared so ISAF have had to make minor changes in the last three years even though the rules are normally not changed in the 4 years between the Olympic Games.

Many rules have now had minor editorial changes to the wording but the 'game' has basically not been changed except maybe by the restraint put on a right-of-way boat by new Rule 16.2.

The following is a summary of the most important changes between the 1997–2000 rulebook and the new 2001–2004 rulebook.

❑ New Rule 16.2 intending to curtail 'hunting' was introduced 1 January 2000. The term 'hunting' is new to many sailors. A right-of-way boat that changes course so as to make it more difficult for another boat to *keep clear* is said to be 'hunting' the other boat. Under the old rules, when a right-of-way boat changed course she was not permitted to **prevent** the other boat from keeping clear, nor was she allowed to **obstruct** the other boat while she was keeping clear. Even if the old requirement not to **obstruct** the other boat did not specifically prohibit a change of course from the right-of-way boat, it was thought to prevent 'hunting'.

The new simplified rules were introduced in 1997, however, with no special 'anti-hunting' rule. A debate about the necessity of such a rule has been going on within ISAF for several years both before and after the introduction of the new rules. Some felt that new Rule 16 by itself provided sufficient control over hunting. Others, especially from North America, argued that new Rule 16 encouraged aggressive tactics like those used in match racing, and that this was directly in conflict with the goals of the new rules to discourage contact and minimise anxiety at close quarters.

Rule 16.2 does not apply to match racing, and some felt that even in a fleet race it puts more restraint on the tactical possibilities of a right-of-way boat than the old requirement not to **obstruct** the other boat.

❏ Rule 17.1 now does not apply if the overlap begins while the windward boat is required to keep clear by Rule 13 ie if she is 'tacking' and not yet on a close-hauled course. This makes it difficult to tack very close on top of another boat ('slam-dunk') because the leeward boat can almost always luff.

❏ Rule 18: After the introduction of the new simple rules in 1997 it quickly became clear that Rule 18 had some unforeseen and undesired loopholes. It has proved very difficult to write a simple rule that will cover all the situations that can arise when rounding marks and obstructions. Marks can be windward, leeward or gybing marks. They are rounded sometimes to starboard sometimes to port and often one or more boats gybe or tack while rounding.

Minor changes were made in December 1998 and December 1999 and with the 2001 edition of the rules, Rule 18 has again been re-edited. However no change to 'the game' is intended and hopefully the new Rule 18 will prove better than the 1997 version.

❏ Rule 26 Starting Races: The old starting system of two Yellow, Blue and Red flags or shapes has gone.

To make the work easier for the Race Committee, the Preparatory signal will now be only one flag: flag P if no start rule is in effect and flag I, flag Z or Black flag if one of these start rules is in effect. No matter which preparatory flag is set, it will be removed with one sound one-minute before the start so there will always be one sound one minute before the start even when no start rule is in effect.

❏ Rule 30.3: The Black flag disqualification rule now makes it clear that if the race is postponed or abandoned *before* the starting signal, boats that are in the forbidden triangle are *not* disqualified. So if the Race Committee can see that the start is going to be a mess, not because the sailors are pushing but, for example, because the starting line is favoured at one end, they can postpone right up to the starting gun and nobody will be disqualified.

❏ New Rule 32.2 makes it clear that the Race Committee can shorten the course to get more races in.

❏ New Rule 60.4 allows the Protest Committee to protest any boat involved when it receives a report (even an invalid protest) that an incident may have resulted in serious damage or injury.

❏ Rule 61.1 Requirements when Protesting has been changed so that boats with a hull length less than 6 metres need not display a flag when protesting and a hail is not needed when the protested boat is beyond hailing distance.

❏ Rule 88.3(b) now makes it clear what happens with the scoring when a disqualification is not excludable (DNE) and the scoring system provides for one or more races being excluded.

❏ Appendix A Scoring has been entirely revised and reworded.

❏ Appendices C and D have been revised and reworded. Match and team racing have used a set of 'Standard Sailing Instructions'. These have been developed and improved during the last four years and these changes are now incorporated in the new Appendices.

❏ Old appendices: G Advertising, K Competitors' ISAF Eligibility and L Banned Substances and Banned Methods have been renamed Appendices 1, 2 and 3 and turned into 'ISAF Regulations'.

ISAF Regulations can be changed whenever necessary, not just every four years so in order to be sure to have the correct version of these regulations one should always look for the latest edition on the ISAF Website:
www. sailing.org/regulations/isafcodes.html

❏ The remaining appendices have been re-allocated letters to keep the lettering in alphabetical order.

❏ Old appendices M (NoR and SI) and N (SI Guide) are therefore now J and K respectively and are slightly changed to make it clearer which rules apply to an event.

❏ There is a new Appendix N advising on how Rule 42 Propulsion is to be enforced on the water. Most sailors already know the principles.

# BRIEF NOTES OF GUIDANCE FOR MAKING A PROTEST

**1** Following an incident you must quickly reach a decision – are you in the wrong? In which case you must either retire or accept a penalty. Or are you the aggrieved boat? In which case you must protest (Rule 60.1). Of course, if the other boat retires or accepts a penalty as a result of this infringement, a protest will not be necessary. But do not come ashore and grumble about the foul and fail to protest.

**2** Be sure in your mind that having decided to protest you have a) tried to inform the other boat (a hail is mandatory if the incident is in the racing area) and b) displayed a protest flag at the first reasonable opportunity (Rule 61.1(a)).

**3** Immediately try to identify any possible witnesses from nearby boats.

**4** After the incident quickly go over the events that led up to the infringement so as to be quite clear about the manner in which it happened. If it is possible, scribble some notes to remind you later about the exact details. Discuss it briefly with your crew if you think it will help. However you should be careful not to spend to much time on the incident while still racing as this could impair your performance.

**5** Be sure that the Race Committee acknowledges your intention to protest as you finish (Rule 61.1(a)).

**6** Once ashore you have several tasks to complete before lodging the protest:

(a) Check the latest time for lodging a Protest (Rule 61.3). It is usually two hours after the last boat finishing but can be varied by the Sailing Instructions. The Protest Time is usually posted on the Official Notice Board; check the Sailing Instructions.

(b) Again be sure that you have tried to inform the protested boat.

(c) Contact your possible witnesses and ask them to attend the hearing if you feel they will support your case. Make sure that your witnesses will be positive to your case in their testimony. Simply padding out your case with a large number of witnesses who have little to add to the facts will do nothing but keep everybody in the Protest Room longer than they wish and may alienate the Protest Committee. Do not rehearse your witness. It is usually very obvious that he or she has been set up in your favour and this may legislate against you.

(d) Think the incident through again. By now, you should be in a position to set out the incident as you saw it and the rest of the contents, on the Protest Form (Rule 61.2). A standard protest form is usually supplied at the Race Office. If not, any sheet of paper will do, provided it is not tatty or soggy; the Protest Committee have to read it. Do not put too much detail on the Protest Form. You can find details of what is required in Rule 61.2. A short description of the incident is all that is necessary. Add details of where and when it took place to make sure everybody knows exactly which incident you are referring to. There may have been several. If possible, add a note of which Rules you think have been infringed. A clear diagram is usually very helpful. (Use the 'ruler' with the models in the front wallet).

(e) One final point to consider, before lodging your protest: if the onus is on you to prove your case, and there is no positive witness in your favour and the evidence is poor, think very carefully before lodging the protest. You have to have a very good case, otherwise it is a lost cause. Such circumstances are:

(i) An outside boat has to satisfy the Protest Committee that she was clear ahead at the moment she reached the two boat length zone around a mark (Rule 18.2(e)).

(ii) An inside boat has to satisfy the Protest Committee that she established her overlap in time (Rule 18.2(e)).

**7** Now lodge the protest. No action can be taken by the Protest Committee to hear your protest unless you lodge it within the required time limit. Remember, once you have lodged a protest it must be heard unless the Protest Committee approves your request to have it withdrawn. (Rule 63.1).

**8** Make sure you know where and when your protest is to be heard. The Sailing Instructions should detail where the notice will be posted.

**9** During the hearing, which should follow the procedure set out in Appendix L, treat the Protest Committee with respect. They will almost certainly be sailors like yourself, doing their best for everybody concerned. Do not be rude or lose your temper. It will do nothing to further your case.

**10** In establishing your case it is often helpful to work back from the incident. The facts as you see them will come out during the hearing. The following table of the rate of advance of a boat may be a helpful guideline in establishing distances.

$$1 \text{ kt} = 0.51 \text{ m/sec}$$
$$2 \text{kt} = 1.03 \text{ m/sec}$$
$$3 \text{kt} = 1.54 \text{ m/sec}$$
$$4 \text{kt} = 2.11 \text{ m/sec}$$
$$5 \text{kt} = 2.57 \text{ m/sec}$$
$$6 \text{kt} = 3.09 \text{ m/sec}$$
$$7 \text{kt} = 3.60 \text{ m/sec}$$
$$8 \text{kt} = 4.12 \text{ m/sec}$$
$$9 \text{kt} = 4.63 \text{ m/sec}$$
$$10 \text{kt} = 5.14 \text{ m/sec}$$

**11** Remember there is no substitute for care in the preparation of your case.

**12** A point for Protest Committees – it is very helpful to the competitor if you give some explanation of the background when you announce your decision. Not only will the competitor learn from that, but it will go a long way towards maintaining the good spirit of the event.

THE
# RACING RULES
OF
# SAILING
## for 2001–2004

## CONTENTS

|  |  | Introduction | 16 |
|---|---|---|---|
|  |  | **Basic Principles: Sportsmanship** |  |
|  |  | **and the Rules** | 17 |
|  |  | **Definitions** | 17 |
| **Part 1** |  | **Fundamental Rules** | 19 |
|  | 1 | Safety | 19 |
|  | 2 | Fair Sailing | 19 |
|  | 3 | Acceptance of the Rules | 19 |
|  | 4 | Decision to Race | 19 |
|  | 5 | Drugs | 19 |
| **Part 2** |  | **When Boats Meet** | 20 |
|  | 10–13 | Section A – Right of Way | 20 |
|  | 14–17 | Section B – General Limitations | 20 |
|  | 18–19 | Section C – At Marks and Obstructions | 21 |
|  | 20–22 | Section D – Other Rules | 24 |
| **Part 3** |  | **Conduct of a Race** | 25 |
|  | 25 | Sailing Instructions and Signals | 25 |
|  | 26 | Starting Races | 25 |
|  | 27 | Other Race Committee Actions before the Starting Signal | 25 |
|  | 28 | Sailing the Course | 26 |
|  | 29 | Starting; Recalls | 26 |
|  | 30 | Starting Penalties | 27 |
|  | 31 | Touching a Mark | 27 |
|  | 32 | Shortening or Abandoning after the Start | 28 |
|  | 33 | Changing the Position of the next Mark | 28 |
|  | 34 | Mark Missing | 28 |
|  | 35 | Time Limit and Scores | 29 |
|  | 36 | Races to be Restarted or Resailed | 29 |

| | | | |
|---|---|---|---|
| **Part 4** | | **Other Requirements When Racing** | 30 |
| | 40 | Personal Buoyancy | 30 |
| | 41 | Outside Help | 30 |
| | 42 | Propulsion | 30 |
| | 43 | Competitor Clothing and Equipment | 31 |
| | 44 | Penalties for Breaking Rules of Part 2 | 32 |
| | 45 | Hauling out; Making Fast; Anchoring | 33 |
| | 46 | Person in Charge | 33 |
| | 47 | Limitations on Equipment and Crew | 33 |
| | 48 | Fog Signals and Lights | 33 |
| | 49 | Crew Position | 33 |
| | 50 | Setting and Sheeting Sails | 34 |
| | 51 | Movable Ballast | 35 |
| | 52 | Manual Power | 35 |
| | 53 | Skin Friction | 35 |
| | 54 | Forestays and Headsail Tacks | 35 |
| **Part 5** | | **Protests, Redress, Hearings, Misconduct and Appeals** | 36 |
| | 60–62 | Section A – Protests and Redress | 36 |
| | 63–68 | Section B – Hearings and Decisions | 38 |
| | 69 | Section C – Gross Misconduct | 42 |
| | 70–71 | Section D – Appeals | 43 |
| **Part 6** | | **Entry and Qualification** | 45 |
| | 75 | Entering a Race | 45 |
| | 76 | Exclusion of Boats and Competitors | 45 |
| | 77 | Identification on Sails | 45 |
| | 78 | Compliance with Class Rules; Certificates | 45 |
| | 79 | Advertising | 46 |
| | 80 | Rescheduled Races | 46 |
| **Part 7** | | **Race Organization** | 47 |
| | 85 | Governing Rules | 47 |
| | 86 | Rule Changes | 47 |
| | 87 | Organizing Authority; Notice of Race; Apointment of Race Officials | 47 |
| | 88 | Race Committee; Sailing Instructions; Scoring | 48 |
| | 89 | Protest Committee | 48 |

# Contents

|  | Appendices Section I | 50 |
|---|---|---|
| Appendix A | Scoring | 50 |
| A1 | Number of Races | 50 |
| A2 | Series Scores | 50 |
| A3 | Starting Times and Finishing Places | 50 |
| A4 | Low Point and Bonus Point Systems | 50 |
| A5 | Scores Determined by the Race Committee | 55 |
| A6 | Changes in Places and Scores of Other Boats | 51 |
| A7 | Race Ties | 51 |
| A8 | Series Ties | 52 |
| A9 | Race Scores in a Series longer than a Regatta | 52 |
| A10 | Guidance on Redress | 52 |
| A11 | Scoring Abbreviations | 53 |
| Appendix B | Sailboard Racing Rules | 53 |
| Appendix C | Match Racing Rules | 55 |
| Appendix D | Team Racing Rules | 65 |
| Appendix E | Radio-Controlled Boat Racing Rules | 69 |
| Appendix F | Appeals Procedure | 76 |
| Appendix G | Identification on Sails | 77 |
| Appendix H | Weighing Clothing and Equipment | 81 |
| Appendix J | Notice of Race and Sailing Instructions | 82 |
| Appendix K | Sailing Instructions Guide | 86 |
| Appendix L | Recommendations for Protest Commitees | 102 |
| Appendix M | International Juries | 106 |
| Appendix N | Immediate Penalties for Breaking Rule 42 | 108 |
|  | Appendices Section II | 110 |
| Appendix 1 | ISAF Advertising Code | 110 |
| Appendix 2 | ISAF Eligibility Code | 117 |
| Appendix 3 | ISAF Anti-doping Code | 120 |
|  | Protest Form | 132 |
|  | Race Signals | 223 |

# INTRODUCTION

*The Racing Rules of Sailing* includes two main sections. The first, Parts 1–7, contains rules that affect all competitors. The second section contains appendices that provide details of rules, rules that apply to particular kinds of racing, and rules that affect only a small number of competitors or officials.

**Revision**   The racing rules are revised and published every four years by the International Sailing Federation (ISAF), the international authority for the sport. This edition becomes effective on 1 April 2001. With the exception of Appendices 1, 2 and 3, changes to the racing rules are permitted under ISAF Regulations 11.2 and 11.3. No changes are contemplated before 2005, but any changes determined to be urgent before then will be announced through national authorities and posted on the ISAF website (www.sailing.org).

**ISAF Codes**   New Appendices 1, 2 and 3 contain the ISAF Advertising Code, the ISAF Eligibility Code and the ISAF Anti-Doping Code, which replace former Appendices G, K and L. These codes are ISAF regulations and are also racing rules. For more information see the preamble to Appendices, Section II.

**Terminology**   A term used in the sense stated in the Definitions is printed in italics or, in preambles, in bold italics (for example, *racing* and **racing**). Other words and terms are used in the sense ordinarily understood in nautical or general use. 'Race committee' includes any person or committee performing a race committee function. 'Class rules' includes rules of handicapping and rating systems.

**Appendices**   When the rules of an appendix apply, they take precedence over any conflicting rules in Parts 1–7. Each appendix is identified by a letter or a number. A reference to a rule in a lettered appendix will contain the letter of the appendix and the rule number (for example, 'rule A1'). There is no Appendix I. A reference to Appendix 1, 2 or 3 will contain the number of the appendix and the regulation number; for example, 'Appendix 1, Regulation 20.1'.

**Changes to the Rules**   The prescriptions of a national authority, class rules or the sailing instructions may change a racing rule only as permitted by rule 86.

# BASIC PRINCIPLE

### SPORTSMANSHIP AND THE RULES

Competitors in the sport of sailing are governed by a body of *rules* that they are expected to follow and enforce. A fundamental principle of sportsmanship is that when competitors break a *rule* they will promptly take a penalty or retire.

143

# DEFINITIONS

*A term used as stated below is shown in italic type or, in preambles, in bold italic type.*

**Abandon**   A race that a race committee or protest committee *abandons* is void but may be resailed.

**Clear Astern** and **Clear Ahead; Overlap**   One boat is *clear astern* of another when her hull and equipment in normal position are behind a line abeam from the aftermost point of the other boat's hull and equipment in normal position. The other boat is *clear ahead.* They *overlap* when neither is *clear astern* or when a boat between them *overlaps* both. These terms do not apply to boats on opposite *tacks* unless rule 18 applies.

137

**Finish**   A boat *finishes* when any part of her hull, or crew or equipment in normal position, crosses the finishing line in the direction of the course from the last *mark,* either for the first time or after taking a penalty under rule 31.2 or 44.2 or, under rule 28.1, after correcting an error made at the finishing line.

138
139
185

**Interested Party**   A person who may gain or lose as a result of a protest committee's decision, or who has a close personal interest in the decision.

**Keep Clear**   One boat *keeps clear* of another if the other can sail her course with no need to take avoiding action and, when the boats are *overlapped* on the same *tack,* if the *leeward* boat can change course in both directions without immediately making contact with the *windward* boat.

**Leeward** and **Windward**   A boat's *leeward* side is the side that is or, when she is head to wind, was away from the wind. However, when sailing by the lee or directly downwind, her *leeward* side is the side on which her mainsail lies. The other side is her *windward* side. When two boats on the same *tack overlap,* the one on the *leeward* side of the other is the *leeward* boat. The other is the *windward* boat.

page
187
141

**Mark**   An object the sailing instructions require a boat to leave on a specified side, and a race committee vessel surrounded by navigable water from which the starting or finishing line extends. An anchor line and objects attached temporarily or accidentally to a *mark* are not part of it.

**Obstruction**   An object that a boat could not pass without changing course substantially, if she were sailing directly towards it and one of her hull lengths from it. An object that can be safely passed on only one side and an area so designated by the sailing instructions are also *obstructions*. However, a boat *racing* is not an *obstruction* to other boats unless they are required to *keep clear* of her, give her *room* or, if rule 21 applies, avoid her.

**Overlap**   See **Clear Astern** and **Clear Ahead; Overlap**.

**Party**   A *party* to a hearing: a protestor; a protestee; a boat requesting redress; a boat or a competitor that may be penalized under rule 69.1; a race committee in a hearing under rule 62.1(a).

141
149

**Postpone**   A *postponed* race is delayed before its scheduled start but may be started or *abandoned* later.

**Proper Course**   A course a boat would sail to *finish* as soon as possible in the absence of the other boats referred to in the rule using the term. A boat has no *proper course* before her starting signal.

139
187

**Protest**   An allegation made under rule 61.2 by a boat, a race committee or a protest committee that a boat has broken a *rule*.

164

**Racing**   A boat is *racing* from her preparatory signal until she *finishes* and clears the finishing line and *marks* or retires, or until the race committee signals a general recall, *postponement* or *abandonment*.

142

**Room**   The space a boat needs in the existing conditions while manoeuvring promptly in a seamanlike way.

**Rule**   (a)   The rules in this book, including the Definitions, Race Signals, Introduction, preambles and the rules of relevant appendices, but not titles;
(b)   the prescriptions of the national authority, unless the sailing instructions state that they do not apply;
(c)   the class rules, or the rules of the handicapping or rating system, except any that conflict with the rules in this book;

142

(d)   the notice of race;
(e)   the sailing instructions; and
(f)   any other documents that govern the event.

140

**Start**   A boat *starts* when after her starting signal any part of her hull, crew or equipment first crosses the starting line and she has complied with rule 29.1 and rule 30.1 if it applies.

140

**Tack, Starboard or Port**   A boat is on the *tack, starboard* or *port*, corresponding to her *windward* side.

**Two-Length Zone**   The area around a *mark* or *obstruction* within a distance of two hull lengths of the boat nearer to it.

**Windward**   See **Leeward** and **Windward**.

# PART 1 – FUNDAMENTAL RULES

page

**1 SAFETY**

**1.1 Helping Those in Danger** 144
A boat or competitor shall give all possible help to any person or vessel in danger.

**1.2 Life-Saving Equipment and Personal Buoyancy** 144
A boat shall carry adequate life-saving equipment for all persons on board, including one item ready for immediate use, unless her class rules make some other provision. Each competitor is individually responsible for wearing personal buoyancy adequate for the conditions.

**2 FAIR SAILING** 144
A boat and her owner shall compete in compliance with recognized principles of sportsmanship and fair play. A boat may be penalized under this rule only if it is clearly established that these principles have been violated. A disqualification under this rule shall not be excluded from the boat's series score.

**3 ACCEPTANCE OF THE RULES** 144
By participating in a race conducted under these racing rules, each competitor and boat owner agrees

(a) to be governed by the *rules*;
(b) to accept the penalties imposed and other action taken under the *rules*, subject to the appeal and review procedures provided in them, as the final determination of any matter arising under the *rules*; and
(c) with respect to such determination, not to resort to any court or other tribunal not provided by the *rules*.

**4 DECISION TO RACE** 144
The responsibility for a boat's decision to participate in a race or to continue *racing* is hers alone.

**5 DRUGS** 144
A competitor shall neither take a substance nor use a method banned by the Olympic Movement Anti-Doping Code or the World Anti-Doping Agency and shall comply with Appendix 3 (ISAF Regulation 19, ISAF Anti-Doping Code). An alleged or actual breach of this rule shall be dealt with under Regulation 19. It shall not be grounds for a *protest* and rule 63.1 does not apply.

(Numbers 6–9 are spare numbers)

# PART 2 – WHEN BOATS MEET

145

*The rules of Part 2 apply between boats that are sailing in or near the racing area and intend to **race**, are **racing**, or have been **racing**. However, a boat not **racing** shall not be penalized for breaking one of these rules, except rule 22.1. The* International Regulations for Preventing Collisions at Sea *or government right-of-way rules apply between a boat sailing under these rules and a vessel that is not, and they replace these rules if the sailing instructions so state.*

## Section A – Right of Way

*A boat has right of way when another boat is required to **keep clear** of her. However, some rules in Sections B, C and D limit the actions of a right-of-way boat.*

146   10   **ON OPPOSITE TACKS**
When boats are on opposite *tacks,* a *port-tack* boat shall *keep clear* of a *starboard-tack* boat.

147   11   **ON THE SAME TACK, OVERLAPPED**
When boats are on the same *tack* and *overlapped,* a *windward* boat shall *keep clear* of a *leeward* boat.

149   12   **ON THE SAME TACK, NOT OVERLAPPED**
When boats are on the same *tack* and not *overlapped,* a boat *clear astern* shall *keep clear* of a boat *clear ahead.*

150   13   **WHILE TACKING**
After a boat passes head to wind, she shall *keep clear* of other boats until she is on a close-hauled course. During that time rules 10, 11 and 12 do not apply. If two boats are subject to this rule at the same time, the one on the other's port side shall *keep clear.*

## Section B – General Limitations

152   14   **AVOIDING CONTACT**
A boat shall avoid contact with another boat if reasonably possible. However, a right-of-way boat or one entitled to *room*

20

(a)  need not act to avoid contact until it is clear that the other boat is not *keeping clear* or giving *room*, and

(b)  shall not be penalized under this rule unless there is contact that causes damage.

## 15  ACQUIRING RIGHT OF WAY

152

When a boat acquires right of way, she shall initially give the other boat *room* to *keep clear*, unless she acquires right of way because of the other boat's actions.

## 16  CHANGING COURSE

156

**16.1**  When a right-of-way boat changes course, she shall give the other boat *room* to *keep clear*.

**16.2**  In addition, when after the starting signal boats are about to cross or are crossing each other on opposite *tacks*, and the *port-tack* boat is *keeping clear* of the *starboard-tack* boat, the *starboard-tack* boat shall not change course if as a result the *port-tack* boat would immediately need to change course to continue *keeping clear*.

## 17  ON THE SAME TACK; PROPER COURSE

158

**17.1**  If a boat *clear astern* becomes *overlapped* within two of her hull lengths to *leeward* of a boat on the same *tack*, she shall not sail above her *proper course* while they remain *overlapped* within that distance, unless in doing so she promptly sails astern of the other boat. This rule does not apply if the *overlap* begins while the *windward* boat is required by rule 13 to *keep clear*.

**17.2**  Except on a beat to windward, while a boat is less than two of her hull lengths from a *leeward* boat or a boat *clear astern* steering a course to *leeward* of her, she shall not sail below her *proper course* unless she gybes.

159

# Section C – At Marks and Obstructions

161

*To the extent that a Section C rule conflicts with a rule in Section A or B, the Section C rule takes precedence.*

## 18  ROUNDING AND PASSING MARKS AND OBSTRUCTIONS

*In rule 18, **room** is room for an inside boat to round or pass between an outside boat and a **mark** or **obstruction**, including **room** to tack or gybe when either is a normal part of the manoeuvre.*

page
162

162

163

**18.1    When This Rule Applies**

Rule 18 applies when boats are about to round or pass a *mark* they are required to leave on the same side, or an *obstruction* on the same side, until they have passed it. However, it does not apply

(a)    at a starting *mark* surrounded by navigable water or at its anchor line from the time the boats are approaching them to *start* until they have passed them, or

(b)    between boats on opposite *tacks*, either on a beat to windward or when the *proper course* for one or both of them to round or pass the *mark* or *obstruction* is to tack.

**18.2    Giving Room; Keeping Clear**

164

(a)    OVERLAPPED – BASIC RULE

When boats are *overlapped* the outside boat shall give the inside boat *room* to round or pass the *mark* or *obstruction,* and if the inside boat has right of way the outside boat shall also *keep clear.* Other parts of rule 18 contain exceptions to this rule.

166

(b)    OVERLAPPED AT THE ZONE

If boats were *overlapped* before either of them reached the *two-length zone* and the *overlap* is broken after one of them has reached it, the boat that was on the outside shall continue to give the other boat *room.* If the outside boat becomes *clear astern* or *overlapped* inside the other boat, she is not entitled to *room* and shall *keep clear.*

169

(c)    NOT OVERLAPPED AT THE ZONE

If a boat is *clear ahead* at the time she reaches the *two-length zone*, the boat *clear astern* shall thereafter *keep clear.* If the boat *clear astern* becomes *overlapped* outside the other boat she shall also give the inside boat *room.* If the boat *clear astern* becomes *overlapped* inside the other boat she is not entitled to *room.* If the boat that was *clear ahead* passes head to wind, rule 18.2(c) no longer applies.

169

(d)    CHANGING COURSE TO ROUND OR PASS

When rule 18 applies between two boats and the right-of-way boat is changing course to round or pass a *mark,* rule 16 does not apply between her and the other boat.

171
169

(e)    OVERLAP RIGHTS

If there is reasonable doubt that a boat obtained or broke an *overlap* in time, it shall be presumed that she did not. If the outside boat is unable to give *room* when an *overlap* begins, rules 18.2(a) and 18.2(b) do not apply.

page

### 18.3 Tacking at a Mark

171

If two boats were approaching a *mark* on opposite *tacks* and one of them completes a tack in the *two-length zone* when the other is fetching the *mark*, rule 18.2 does not apply. The boat that tacked

(a) shall not cause the other boat to sail above close-hauled to avoid her or prevent the other boat from passing the *mark*, and

171

(b) shall give *room* if the other boat becomes *overlapped* inside her, in which case rule 15 does not apply.

172

### 18.4 Gybing

173

When an inside *overlapped* right-of-way boat must gybe at a *mark* or *obstruction* to sail her *proper course*, until she gybes she shall sail no farther from the *mark* or *obstruction* than needed to sail that course.

### 18.5 Passing a Continuing Obstruction

174

While boats are passing a continuing *obstruction*, rules 18.2(b) and 18.2(c) do not apply. A boat *clear astern* that obtains an inside *overlap* is entitled to *room* to pass between the other boat and the *obstruction* only if at the moment the *overlap* begins there is *room* to do so. If there is not, she is not entitled to *room* and shall *keep clear*.

### 19 ROOM TO TACK AT AN OBSTRUCTION

175

19.1 When safety requires a close-hauled boat to make a substantial course change to avoid an *obstruction* and she intends to tack, but cannot tack and avoid another boat on the same *tack*, she shall hail for *room* to do so. Before tacking she shall give the hailed boat time to respond. The hailed boat shall either

(a) tack as soon as possible, in which case the hailing boat shall also tack as soon as possible, or

(b) immediately reply 'You tack', in which case the hailing boat shall tack as soon as possible and the hailed boat shall give *room*, and rules 10 and 13 do not apply.

19.2 Rule 19.1 does not apply at a starting *mark* surrounded by navigable water or at its anchor line from the time boats are approaching them to *start* until they have passed them or at a

177

page

*mark* that the hailed boat can fetch. When rule 19.1 applies, rule 18 does not.

## Section D – Other Rules

*When rule 20 or 21 applies between two boats, Section A rules do not.*

179

**20     STARTING ERRORS; PENALTY TURNS; MOVING ASTERN**
A boat sailing towards the pre-start side of the starting line or its extensions after her starting signal to comply with rule 29.1 or 30.1 shall *keep clear* of a boat not doing so until she is completely on the pre-start side. A boat making a penalty turn shall *keep clear* of one that is not. A boat moving astern by backing a sail shall *keep clear* of one that is not.

182
182

183

**21     CAPSIZED, ANCHORED OR AGROUND; RESCUING**
If possible, a boat shall avoid a boat that is capsized or has not regained control after capsizing, is anchored or aground, or is trying to help a person or vessel in danger. A boat is capsized when her masthead is in the water.

**22      INTERFERING WITH ANOTHER BOAT**

**22.1**   If reasonably possible, a boat not *racing* shall not interfere with a boat that is *racing.*

**22.2**   A boat shall not deliberately interfere with a boat making penalty turns to delay her.


(Numbers 23–24 are spare numbers)

# PART 3 – CONDUCT OF A RACE

page

**25  SAILING INSTRUCTIONS AND SIGNALS**    187

Sailing instructions shall be made available to each boat before a race begins. The meanings of the visual and sound signals stated in Race Signals shall not be changed except under rule 86.1(b). The meanings of any other signals that may be used shall be stated in the sailing instructions.

**26  STARTING RACES**    187

Races shall be started by using the following signals. Times shall be taken from the visual signals; the absence of a sound signal shall be disregarded.

| Signal | Flag and sound | Minutes before starting signal |
|---|---|---|
| Warning | Class flag; 1 sound | 5* |
| Preparatory | P, I, Z, Z with I, or black flag; 1 sound | 4 |
| One-minute | Preparatory flag removed; 1 long sound | 1 |
| Starting | Class flag removed; 1 sound | 0 |

* or as stated in the sailing instructions

The warning signal for each succeeding class shall be made with or after the starting signal of the preceding class.

**27  OTHER RACE COMMITTEE ACTIONS BEFORE THE STARTING SIGNAL**

**27.1**  No later than the warning signal, the race committee shall signal or otherwise designate the course to be sailed if the sailing instructions have not stated the course, and it may replace one course signal with another, signal that a designated short course will be used (display flag S with two sounds), and signal that wearing personal buoyancy is required (display flag Y with one sound).

**27.2**  No later than the preparatory signal, the race committee may move a starting *mark* and may apply rule 30.

**27.3**  Before the starting signal, the race committee may for any reason *postpone* (display flag AP, AP over H, or AP over A, with two sounds) or *abandon* the race (display flag N over H, or N over A, with three sounds).

**28    SAILING THE COURSE**

**28.1**    A boat shall *start,* leave each *mark* on the required side in the correct order, and *finish,* so that a string representing her wake after *starting* and until *finishing* would when drawn taut pass each *mark* on the required side and touch each rounding *mark.* After *finishing* she need not cross the finishing line completely. She may correct any errors to comply with this rule, provided she has not already *finished.*

**28.2**    A boat may leave on either side a *mark* that does not begin, bound or end the leg she is on. However, she shall leave a starting *mark* on the required side when she is approaching the starting line from its pre-start side to *start.*

**29    STARTING; RECALLS**

**29.1    On the Course Side at the Start**
When at a boat's starting signal any part of her hull, crew or equipment is on the course side of the starting line, she shall sail completely to the pre-start side of the line before *starting.*

**29.2    Individual Recall**
When at a boat's starting signal she must comply with rule 29.1 or 30.1, the race committee shall promptly display flag X with one sound. The flag shall be displayed until all such boats are completely on the pre-start side of the starting line or its extensions and have complied with rule 30.1 if it applies, but not later than four minutes after the starting signal or one minute before any later starting signal, whichever is earlier.

**29.3    General Recall**
When at the starting signal the race committee is unable to identify boats that are on the course side of the starting line or to which rule 30 applies, or there has been an error in the starting procedure, the race committee may signal a general recall (display the First Substitute with two sounds). The warning signal for a new start for the recalled class shall be made one minute after the First Substitute is removed (one sound), and the starts for any succeeding classes shall follow the new start.

*page* 184, 186, 187

## 30 STARTING PENALTIES

### 30.1 Round-an-End Rule

If flag I has been displayed before, with, or as a boat's preparatory signal, and any part of her hull, crew or equipment is on the course side of the starting line or its extensions during the minute before her starting signal, she shall sail to the pre-start side of the line around either end before *starting.*

### 30.2 20% Penalty Rule

If flag Z has been displayed before, with, or as a boat's preparatory signal, no part of her hull, crew or equipment shall be in the triangle formed by the ends of the starting line and the first *mark* during the minute before her starting signal. If a boat breaks this rule and is identified, she shall receive, without a hearing, a 20% scoring penalty calculated as stated in rule 44.3(c). She shall be penalized even if the race is restarted, resailed or rescheduled, but not if it is *postponed* or *abandoned* before the starting signal.

### 30.3 Black Flag Rule

If a black flag has been displayed before, with, or as a boat's preparatory signal, no part of her hull, crew or equipment shall be in the triangle formed by the ends of the starting line and the first *mark* during the minute before her starting signal. If a boat breaks this rule and is identified, she shall be disqualified without a hearing, even if the race is restarted, resailed or rescheduled, but not if it is *postponed* or *abandoned* before the starting signal. If a general recall is signalled or the race is *abandoned* after the starting signal, the race committee shall display her sail number, and if the race is restarted or resailed she shall not sail in it. If she does so, her disqualification shall not be excluded in calculating her series score.

187

## 31 TOUCHING A MARK

### 31.1 While *racing,* a boat shall not touch a starting *mark* before *starting,* a *mark* that begins, bounds or ends the leg of the course on which she is sailing, or a finishing *mark* after *finishing.*

187

### 31.2 A boat that has broken rule 31.1 may, after getting well clear of other boats as soon as possible, take a penalty by promptly making one complete 360° turn including one tack and one gybe. When a boat takes the penalty after touching a finishing *mark,* she shall sail completely to the course side of the line

188

189

before *finishing*. However, if a boat has gained a significant advantage in the race or series by touching the *mark* she shall retire.

## 32 SHORTENING OR ABANDONING AFTER THE START

**32.1** After the starting signal, the race committee may *abandon* the race (display flag N, N over H, or N over A, with three sounds) or shorten the course (display flag S with two sounds), as appropriate,

(a) because of an error in the starting procedure,
(b) because of foul weather,
(c) because of insufficient wind making it unlikely that any boat will *finish* within the time limit,
(d) because a *mark* is missing or out of position, or
(e) for any other reason directly affecting the safety or fairness of the competition.

However, after one boat has sailed the course and *finished* within the time limit, if any, the race committee shall not *abandon* the race without considering the consequences for all boats in the race or series.

**32.2** After the starting signal, the race committee may shorten the course (display flag S with two sounds) to enable further scheduled races to be sailed.

## 33 CHANGING THE POSITION OF THE NEXT MARK

At any rounding *mark* the race committee may signal a change of the direction of the next leg of the course by displaying flag C with repetitive sounds and the compass bearing of that leg before any boat begins it. The race committee may change the length of the next leg by displaying flag C with repetitive sounds and a '–' if the leg will be shortened or a '+' if the leg will be lengthened.

## 34 MARK MISSING

When a *mark* is missing or out of position, the race committee shall, if possible,

(a) replace it in its correct position or
(b) substitute one of similar appearance, or a buoy or vessel displaying flag M with repetitive sounds.

35    **TIME LIMIT AND SCORES**                                              page
If one boat sails the course as required by rule 28.1 and *finishes* within the time limit, if any, all boats that *finish* shall be scored according to their finishing places unless the race is *abandoned*. If no boat *finishes* within the time limit, the race committee shall *abandon* the race.

36    **RACES TO BE RESTARTED OR RESAILED**
If a race is restarted or resailed, a breach of a *rule*, other than rule 30.3, in the original race shall not prohibit a boat from competing or, except under rule 30.2, 30.3 or 69, cause her to be penalized.

(Numbers 37–39 are spare numbers)

# PART 4 – OTHER REQUIREMENTS
# WHEN RACING

*Part 4 rules apply only to boats **racing**.*

**40      PERSONAL BUOYANCY**
When flag Y is displayed with one sound before or with the
warning signal, competitors shall wear life-jackets or other
adequate personal buoyancy. Wet suits and dry suits are not
adequate personal buoyancy.

**41      OUTSIDE HELP**
A boat may receive outside help as provided for in rule 1.
Otherwise, she shall not receive help except for an ill or
injured crew member or, after a collision, from the crew of
the other boat.

**42      PROPULSION**

**42.1    Basic Rule**
Except when permitted in rule 42.3 or 45, a boat shall compete by using only the wind and water to increase, maintain
or decrease her speed. Her crew may adjust the trim of sails
and hull, and perform other acts of seamanship, but shall not
otherwise move their bodies to propel the boat.

**42.2    Prohibited Actions**
Without limiting the application of rule 42.1, these actions
are prohibited:

(a)   pumping: repeated fanning of any sail either by trim-
      ming and releasing the sail or by vertical or
      athwartships body movement;
(b)   rocking: repeated rolling of the boat, induced either by
      body movement or adjustment of the sails or centre-
      board, that does not facilitate steering;
(c)   ooching: sudden forward body movement, stopped
      abruptly;
(d)   sculling: repeated movement of the helm not necessary
      for steering;
(e)   repeated tacks or gybes unrelated to changes in the
      wind or to tactical considerations.

## 42.3 Exceptions

(a) A boat's crew may move their bodies to exaggerate the rolling that facilitates steering the boat through a tack or a gybe, provided that, just after the tack or gybe is completed, the boat's speed is not greater than it would have been in the absence of the tack or gybe.

(b) Except on a beat to windward, when surfing (rapidly accelerating down the leeward side of a wave) or planing is possible, the boat's crew may pull the sheet and the guy controlling any sail in order to initiate surfing or planing, but only once for each wave or gust of wind.

(c) Any means of propulsion may be used to help a person or another vessel in danger.

(d) To get clear after grounding or colliding with another boat or object, a boat may use force applied by the crew of either boat and any equipment other than a propulsion engine.

## 43 COMPETITOR CLOTHING AND EQUIPMENT

190

43.1 (a) Competitors shall not wear or carry clothing or equipment for the purpose of increasing their weight.

(b) Furthermore, a competitor's clothing and equipment shall not weigh more than 8 kilograms, excluding a hiking or trapeze harness and clothing (including footwear) worn only below the knee. Class rules or sailing instructions may specify a lower weight or a higher weight up to 10 kilograms. Class rules may include footwear and other clothing worn below the knee within that weight. A hiking or trapeze harness shall have positive buoyancy and shall not weigh more than 2 kilograms, except that class rules may specify a higher weight up to 4 kilograms. Weights shall be determined as required by Appendix H.

(c) When a measurer in charge of weighing clothing and equipment believes a competitor may have broken rule 43.1(a) or 43.1(b) he shall report the matter in writing to the race committee, which shall protest the boat of the competitor.

43.2 Rule 43.1(b) does not apply to boats required to be equipped with lifelines.

**44**     PENALTIES FOR BREAKING RULES OF PART 2

**44.1**  **Taking a Penalty**

A boat that may have broken a rule of Part 2 while *racing* may take a penalty at the time of the incident. Her penalty shall be a 720° Turns Penalty unless the sailing instructions specify the use of the Scoring Penalty or some other penalty. However, if she caused serious damage or gained a significant advantage in the race or series by her breach she shall retire.

**44.2**  **720° Turns Penalty**

After getting well clear of other boats as soon after the incident as possible, a boat takes a 720° Turns Penalty by promptly making two complete 360° turns (720°) in the same direction, including two tacks and two gybes. When a boat takes the penalty at or near the finishing line, she shall sail completely to the course side of the line before *finishing*.

**44.3**  **Scoring Penalty**

(a)  A boat takes a Scoring Penalty by displaying a yellow flag at the first reasonable opportunity after the incident, keeping it displayed until *finishing*, and calling the race committee's attention to it at the finishing line. At that time she shall also inform the race committee of the identity of the other boat involved in the incident. If this is impracticable, she shall do so at the first reasonable opportunity within the time limit for *protests*.

(b)  If a boat displays a yellow flag, she shall also comply with the other parts of rule 44.3(a).

(c)  The boat's penalty score shall be the score for the place worse than her actual finishing place by the number of places stated in the sailing instructions, except that she shall not be scored worse than Did Not Finish. When the sailing instructions do not state the number of places, the number shall be the whole number (rounding 0.5 upward) nearest to 20% of the number of boats entered. The scores of other boats shall not be changed; therefore, two boats may receive the same score.

**44.4**  **Limits on Penalties**

(a)  When a boat intends to take a penalty as provided in rule 44.1 and in the same incident has touched a *mark*, she need not take the penalty provided in rule 31.2.

(b)   A boat that takes a penalty shall not be penalized further with respect to the same incident unless she failed to retire when rule 44.1 required her to do so.

page

**45**   HAULING OUT; MAKING FAST; ANCHORING

190

A boat shall be afloat and off moorings at her preparatory signal. Thereafter, she shall not be hauled out or made fast except to bail out, reef sails or make repairs. She may anchor or the crew may stand on the bottom. She shall recover the anchor before continuing in the race unless she is unable to do so.

217

**46**   PERSON IN CHARGE

A boat shall have on board a person in charge designated by the member or organization that entered the boat. See rule 75.

**47**   LIMITATIONS ON EQUIPMENT AND CREW

**47.1**   A boat shall use only the equipment on board at her preparatory signal.

**47.2**   No person on board shall intentionally leave, except when ill or injured, or to help a person or vessel in danger, or to swim. A person leaving the boat by accident or to swim shall be back on board before the boat continues in the race.

**48**   FOG SIGNALS AND LIGHTS

When safety requires, a boat shall sound fog signals and show lights as required by the *International Regulations for Preventing Collisions at Sea* or applicable government rules.

**49**   CREW POSITION

**49.1**   Competitors shall use no device designed to position their bodies outboard, other than hiking straps and stiffeners worn under the thighs.

**49.2**   When lifelines are required by the class rules or the sailing instructions they shall be taut, and competitors shall not position any part of their torsos outside them, except briefly to perform a necessary task. On boats equipped with upper and lower lifelines of wire, a competitor sitting on the deck facing outboard with his waist inside the lower lifeline may have the upper part of his body outside the upper lifeline.

191

## 50    SETTING AND SHEETING SAILS

### 50.1   Changing Sails
When headsails or spinnakers are being changed, a replacing sail may be fully set and trimmed before the replaced sail is lowered. However, only one mainsail and, except when changing, only one spinnaker shall be carried set at a time.

### 50.2   Spinnaker Poles, Whisker Poles
Only one spinnaker pole or whisker pole shall be used at a time except when gybing. When in use, it shall be attached to the foremost mast.

### 50.3   Use of Outriggers

(a) No sail shall be sheeted over or through an outrigger, except as permitted in rule 50.3(b). An outrigger is any fitting or other device so placed that it could exert outward pressure on a sheet or sail at a point from which, with the boat upright, a vertical line would fall outside the hull or deck planking. For the purpose of this rule, bulwarks, rails and rubbing strakes are not part of the hull or deck planking and the following are not outriggers: a bowsprit used to secure the tack of a working sail, a bumkin used to sheet the boom of a working sail, or a boom of a boomed headsail that requires no adjustment when tacking.

(b) (1) Any sail may be sheeted to or led above a boom that is regularly used for a working sail and is permanently attached to the mast from which the head of the working sail is set.

(2) A headsail may be sheeted or attached at its clew to a spinnaker pole or whisker pole, provided that a spinnaker is not set.

### 50.4   Headsails
The difference between a headsail and a spinnaker is that the mid-girth of a headsail, measured from the mid-points of its luff and leech, does not exceed 50% of the length of its foot, and no other intermediate girth exceeds a percentage similarly proportional to its distance from the head of the sail. A sail tacked down behind the foremost mast is not a headsail.

51    MOVABLE BALLAST
      All movable ballast shall be properly stowed, and water, dead
      weight or ballast shall not be moved for the purpose of
      changing trim or stability. Floorboards, bulkheads, doors,
      stairs and water tanks shall be left in place and all cabin fix-
      tures kept on board.

52    MANUAL POWER
      A boat's standing rigging, running rigging, spars and mov-
      able hull appendages shall be adjusted and operated only by
      manual power.

53    SKIN FRICTION
      A boat shall not eject or release a substance, such as a poly-
      mer, or have specially textured surfaces that could improve
      the character of the flow of water inside the boundary layer.

54    FORESTAYS AND HEADSAIL TACKS
      Forestays and headsail tacks, except those of spinnaker stay-
      sails when the boat is not close-hauled, shall be attached
      approximately on a boat's centre-line.

      (Numbers 55–59 are spare numbers)

page
191

# PART 5 – PROTESTS, REDRESS, HEARINGS, MISCONDUCT AND APPEALS

## Section A – Protests and Redress

**60      RIGHT TO PROTEST AND REQUEST REDRESS**

**60.1**   A boat may

(a)   protest another boat, but not for an alleged breach of a rule of Part 2 unless she was involved in or saw the incident; or

(b)   request redress.

**60.2**   A race committee may

(a)   protest a boat, but not as a result of a report by a competitor from another boat or other *interested party* or of information in an invalid *protest*;

(b)   request redress for a boat; or

(c)   report to the protest committee requesting action under rule 69.1(a).

**60.3**   A protest committee may

(a)   protest a boat, but not as a result of a report by a competitor from another boat or other *interested party* except under rule 61.1(c), or as a result of information in an invalid *protest* except under rule 60.4;

(b)   call a hearing to consider redress; or

(c)   act under rule 69.1(a).

**60.4**   If a protest committee receives a report of an incident that may have resulted in serious damage or serious injury, it may protest any boat involved.

**61      PROTEST REQUIREMENTS**

**61.1**   **Informing the Protestee**

(a)   A boat intending to protest shall always inform the other boat at the first reasonable opportunity. When her

page

*protest* concerns an incident in the racing area that she is involved in or sees, she shall hail 'Protest' and conspicuously display a red flag at the first reasonable opportunity for each. However, boats of hull length less than 6 metres need not display the flag, and if the other boat is beyond hailing distance the protesting boat need not hail but shall inform the other boat at the first reasonable opportunity. A boat required to display a flag shall do so until she is no longer *racing.*

(b)   A race committee or protest committee intending to protest a boat under rule 60.2(a) or 60.3(a) shall inform her as soon as reasonably possible, except that if the *protest* arises from an incident it observes in the racing area the committee shall inform the boat after the race within the time limit of rule 61.3.

(c)   During the hearing of a valid *protest* or request for redress, if the protest committee decides to protest a boat that was involved in the incident but is not a *party* to that hearing, it shall inform the boat as soon as reasonably possible of its intention, then protest her as required by rule 61.2 and proceed with a hearing as required by rule 63.

192

## 61.2   Protest Contents

A *protest* shall be in writing and identify

(a)   the protestor and protestee;
(b)   the incident, including where and when it occurred;
(c)   any *rule* the protestor believes was broken; and
(d)   the name of the protestor's representative.

Provided the written *protest* identifies the incident, other details may be corrected before or during the hearing.

## 61.3   Protest Time Limit

A *protest* by a boat, or by the race committee or protest committee about an incident the committee observes in the racing area, shall be delivered to the race office no later than the time limit stated in the sailing instructions. If none is stated, the time limit is two hours after the last boat in the race *finishes.* Other race committee or protest committee *protests* shall be delivered to the race office within two hours after the committee receives the relevant information. The protest committee shall extend the time if there is good reason to do so.

**62    REDRESS**

**62.1**   A request for redress or a protest committee's decision to consider redress shall be based on a claim or possibility that a boat's finishing place in a race or series has, through no fault of her own, been made significantly worse by

(a)   an improper action or omission of the race committee or protest committee,

(b)   physical damage because of the action of a boat that was breaking a rule of Part 2 or of a vessel not *racing* that was required to keep clear,

(c)   giving help (except to herself or her crew) in compliance with rule 1.1, or

(d)   a boat against which a penalty has been imposed under rule 2 or disciplinary action has been taken under rule 69.1(b).

**62.2**   The request shall be made in writing within the time limit of rule 61.3 or within two hours of the relevant incident, whichever is later. The protest committee shall extend the time if there is good reason to do so. No red flag is required.

## Section B – Hearings and Decisions

**63    HEARINGS**

**63.1    Requirement for a Hearing**
A boat or competitor shall not be penalized without a protest hearing, except as provided in rules 30.2, 30.3, 67, 69, A5 and N2. A decision on redress shall not be made without a hearing. The protest committee shall hear all *protests* and requests for redress that have been delivered to the race office unless it allows a boat to withdraw her *protest* or request.

**63.2    Time and Place of the Hearing; Time for Parties to Prepare**
All *parties* to the hearing shall be notified of the time and place of the hearing, the *protest* or redress information shall be made available to them, and they shall be allowed reasonable time to prepare for the hearing.

**63.3    Right to Be Present**

(a)   The *parties* to the hearing, or a representative of each, have the right to be present throughout the hearing of all

# Rules 62–63

the evidence. When a *protest* claims a breach of a rule of Part 2, 3 or 4, the representatives of boats shall have been on board at the time of the incident, unless there is good reason for the protest committee to rule otherwise. Any witness, other than a member of the protest committee, shall be excluded except when giving evidence.

(b) If a *party* to the hearing does not come to the hearing, the protest committee may nevertheless decide the *protest* or request for redress. If the *party* was unavoidably absent, the committee may reopen the hearing.

**63.4   Interested Party**

A member of a protest committee who is an *interested party* shall not take any further part in the hearing but may appear as a witness. A *party* to the hearing who believes a member of the protest committee is an *interested party* shall object as soon as possible.

**63.5   Validity of the Protest or Request for Redress**

At the beginning of the hearing the protest committee shall decide whether all requirements for the *protest* or request for redress have been met, after first taking any evidence it considers necessary. If all requirements have been met, the *protest* or request is valid and the hearing shall be continued. If not, it shall be closed. If the *protest* has been made under rule 60.4, the protest committee must also determine whether or not serious damage or serious injury resulted from the incident in question. If not, the hearing shall be closed.

**63.6   Taking Evidence and Finding Facts**

The protest committee shall take the evidence of the *parties* to the hearing and of their witnesses and other evidence it considers necessary. A member of the protest committee who saw the incident may give evidence. A *party* to the hearing may question any person who gives evidence. The committee shall then find the facts and base its decision on them.

**63.7   Protests Between Boats in Different Races**

A *protest* between boats sailing in different races conducted by different organizing authorities shall be heard by a protest committee acceptable to those authorities.

## 64    DECISIONS

### 64.1    Penalties and Exoneration

(a)    When the protest committee decides that a boat that is a *party* to a protest hearing has broken a *rule*, it shall disqualify her unless some other penalty applies. A penalty shall be imposed whether or not the applicable *rule* was mentioned in the *protest*.

(b)    When as a consequence of breaking a *rule* a boat has compelled another boat to break a *rule*, rule 64.1(a) does not apply to the other boat and she shall be exonerated.

(c)    If a boat has broken a *rule* when not *racing*, her penalty shall apply to the race sailed nearest in time to that of the incident.

### 64.2    Decisions on Redress

When the protest committee decides that a boat is entitled to redress under rule 62, it shall make as fair an arrangement as possible for all boats affected, whether or not they asked for redress. This may be to adjust the scoring (see rule A10 for some examples) or finishing times of boats, to *abandon* the race, to let the results stand or to make some other arrangement. When in doubt about the facts or probable results of any arrangement for the race or series, especially before *abandoning* the race, the protest committee shall take evidence from appropriate sources.

### 64.3    Decisions on Measurement Protests

(a)    When the protest committee finds that deviations in excess of tolerances specified in the class rules were caused by damage or normal wear and do not improve the performance of the boat, it shall not penalize her. However, the boat shall not *race* again until the deviations have been corrected, except when the protest committee decides there is or has been no reasonable opportunity to do so.

(b)    When the protest committee is in doubt about the meaning of a measurement rule, it shall refer its questions, together with the relevant facts, to an authority responsible for interpreting the rule. In making its decision, the committee shall be bound by the reply of the authority.

(c)    When a boat disqualified under a measurement rule states in writing that she intends to appeal, she may compete in subsequent races without changes to the boat, but will be disqualified if she fails to appeal or the appeal is decided against her.

(d) Measurement costs arising from a *protest* involving a measurement rule shall be paid by the unsuccessful *party* unless the protest committee decides otherwise.

## 65    INFORMING THE PARTIES AND OTHERS

65.1    After making its decision, the protest committee shall promptly inform the *parties* to the hearing of the facts found, the applicable *rules*, the decision, the reasons for it, and any penalties imposed or redress given.

65.2    A *party* to the hearing is entitled to receive the above information in writing, provided she asks for it in writing from the protest committee within seven days of being informed of the decision. The committee shall then promptly provide the information, including, when relevant, a diagram of the incident prepared or endorsed by the committee.

65.3    When the protest committee penalizes a boat under a measurement rule, it shall send the above information to the relevant measurement authorities.

## 66    REOPENING A HEARING
The protest committee may reopen a hearing when it decides that it may have made a significant error, or when significant new evidence becomes available within a reasonable time. It shall reopen a hearing when required by the national authority under rule F5. A *party* to the hearing may ask for a reopening no later than 24 hours after being informed of the decision. When a hearing is reopened, a majority of the members of the protest committee shall, if possible, be members of the original protest committee.

## 67    RULE 42 AND HEARING REQUIREMENT
When so stated in the sailing instructions, the protest committee may penalize without a hearing a boat that has broken rule 42, provided that a member of the committee or its designated observer has seen the incident, and a disqualification under this rule shall not be excluded from the boat's series score. A boat so penalized shall be informed by notification in the race results.

68      **DAMAGES**

The question of damages arising from a breach of any *rule* shall be governed by the prescriptions, if any, of the national authority.

## Section C – Gross Misconduct

**69**      **ALLEGATIONS OF GROSS MISCONDUCT**

**69.1**    **Action by a Protest Committee**

(a)   When a protest committee, from its own observation or a report received, believes that a competitor may have committed a gross breach of a *rule* or of good manners or sportsmanship, or may have brought the sport into disrepute, it may call a hearing. The protest committee shall promptly inform the competitor in writing of the alleged misconduct and of the time and place of the hearing.

(b)   A protest committee of at least three members shall conduct the hearing, following rules 63.2, 63.3, 63.4 and 63.6. If it decides that the competitor committed the alleged misconduct it shall either
(1)   warn the competitor or
(2)   impose a penalty by excluding the competitor, and a boat when appropriate, from a race, or the remaining races of a series or the entire series, or by taking other action within its jurisdiction.

(c)   The protest committee shall promptly report a penalty, but not a warning, to the national authorities of the venue, of the competitor and of the boat owner.

(d)   If the competitor has left the venue and cannot be notified or fails to attend the hearing, the protest committee shall collect all available evidence and, when the allegation seems justified, make a report to the relevant national authorities.

(e)   When the protest committee has left the event and a report alleging misconduct is received, the race committee or organizing authority may appoint a new protest committee to proceed under this rule.

**69.2**    **Action by a National Authority**

(a)   When a national authority receives a report required by rule 69.1(c) or 69.1(d), or a report alleging a gross breach of a *rule* or of good manners or sportsmanship or conduct that brought the sport into disrepute, it may conduct an investigation and, when appropriate, shall conduct a hearing. It may then take any disciplinary action within its jurisdiction it considers appropriate against the competitor or boat, or other person involved, including suspending eligibility, permanently or for a specified period of time, to compete in any event held within its jurisdiction, and suspending ISAF eligibility under Appendix 2, Regulation 21.3.1(a).

(b) The national authority of a competitor shall also suspend the ISAF eligibility of the competitor as required in Appendix 2, Regulation 21.3.1(a).

(c) The national authority shall promptly report a suspension of eligibility under rule 69.2(a) to the ISAF, and to the national authorities of the person or the owner of the boat suspended if they are not members of the suspending national authority.

**69.3    Action by the ISAF**

Upon receipt of a report required by rules 69.2(c) and Appendix 2, Regulation 21.4.1, the ISAF shall inform all national authorities, which may also suspend eligibility for events held within their jurisdiction. The ISAF Executive Committee shall suspend the competitor's ISAF eligibility as required in Appendix 2, Regulation 21.3.1(a) if the competitor's national authority does not do so.

## Section D – Appeals

**70    RIGHT OF APPEAL AND REQUESTS FOR INTERPRETATION**

**70.1**    Provided that the right of appeal has not been denied under rule 70.4, a protest committee's interpretation of a *rule* or its procedures, but not the facts in its decision, may be appealed to the national authority of the venue by

(a) a boat or competitor that is a *party* to a hearing, or

(b) a race committee that is a *party* to a hearing, provided the protest committee is a jury.

193

**70.2**    A protest committee may request confirmation or correction of its decision.

**70.3**    A club or other organization affiliated to a national authority may request an interpretation of the *rules*, provided that no *protest* or request for redress that may be appealed is involved.

**70.4**    There shall be no appeal from the decisions of an international jury constituted in compliance with Appendix M. Furthermore, if the notice of race and the sailing instructions so state, the right of appeal may be denied provided that

(a)    it is essential to determine promptly the result of a race that will qualify a boat to compete in a later stage of an event or a subsequent event (a national authority may prescribe that its approval is required for such a procedure),

(b)    a national authority so approves for a particular event open only to entrants under its own jurisdiction, or

(c)    a national authority after consultation with the ISAF so approves for a particular event, provided the jury is constituted as required by Appendix M, except that only two members of the jury need be International Judges.

**70.5**    Appeals and requests shall conform to Appendix F.

**71**    **APPEAL DECISIONS**

**71.1**    No *interested party* or member of the protest committee shall take any part in the discussion or decision on an appeal or a request for confirmation or correction.

**71.2**    The national authority may uphold, change or reverse the protest committee's decision, declare the *protest* or request for redress invalid, or return the *protest* or request for a new hearing and decision by the same or a different protest committee.

**71.3**    When from the facts found by the protest committee the national authority decides that a boat that was a *party* to a protest hearing broke a *rule*, it shall penalize her, whether or not that boat or that *rule* was mentioned in the protest committee's decision.

**71.4**    The decision of the national authority shall be final. The national authority shall send its decision in writing to all *parties* to the hearing and the protest committee, who shall be bound by the decision.

221

(Numbers 72–74 are spare numbers)

# PART 6 – ENTRY AND QUALIFICATION

## 75 ENTERING A RACE

**75.1** To enter a race, a boat shall comply with the requirements of the organizing authority of the race. She shall be entered by

(a) a member of a club or other organization affiliated to a national authority,
(b) such a club or organization, or
(c) a member of a national authority.

**75.2** Competitors shall comply with Appendix 2.

## 76 EXCLUSION OF BOATS OR COMPETITORS

**76.1** The organizing authority or the race committee may reject or cancel the entry of a boat or exclude a competitor, subject to rule 76.2, provided it does so before the start of the first race and states the reason for doing so. However, the organizing authority or the race committee shall not reject or cancel the entry of a boat or exclude a competitor because of advertising, provided the boat or competitor complies with Appendix 1.

**76.2** At world and continental championships no entry within stated quotas shall be rejected or cancelled without first obtaining the approval of the relevant international class association (or the Offshore Racing Council) or the ISAF.

## 77 IDENTIFICATION ON SAILS
A boat shall comply with the requirements of Appendix G governing class insignia, national letters and numbers on sails.

## 78 COMPLIANCE WITH CLASS RULES; CERTIFICATES

**78.1** A boat's owner and any other person in charge shall ensure that the boat is maintained to comply with her class rules and that her measurement or rating certificate, if any, remains valid.

194

**78.2** When a *rule* requires a certificate to be produced before a boat *races,* and it is not produced, the boat may *race* provided that the race committee receives a statement signed by the person in charge that a valid certificate exists and that it will be given to the race committee before the end of the event. If the certificate is not received in time, the boat's scores shall be removed from the event results.

78.3    When a measurer for an event concludes that a boat or personal equipment does not comply with the class rules, he shall report the matter in writing to the race committee, which shall protest the boat.

79      **ADVERTISING**
A boat and her crew shall comply with Appendix 1.

80      **RESCHEDULED RACES**
When a race has been rescheduled, rule 36 applies and all boats entered in the original race shall be notified and, unless disqualified under rule 30.3, be entitled to sail the rescheduled race. New entries that meet the entry requirements of the original race may be accepted at the discretion of the race committee.

(Numbers 81–84 are spare numbers)

# PART 7 – RACE ORGANIZATION

85     **GOVERNING RULES**

The organizing authority, race committee and protest committee shall be governed by the *rules* in the conduct and judging of races.

86     **RULE CHANGES**        195

86.1    A racing rule may not be changed unless permitted in the rule itself or as follows:

(a)   Prescriptions of a national authority may change a racing rule, but not the Definitions; a rule in the Introduction; Sportsmanship and the Rules; Part 1, 2 or 7; rule 43.1, 43.2, 69, 70, 71, 75, 76.2 or 79; a rule of an appendix that changes one of these rules; or Appendix H, M, 1, 2 or 3.

(b)   Sailing instructions may change a racing rule by referring specifically to it and stating the change, but not rule 76.1, Appendix F, or a rule listed in rule 86.1(a).

(c)   Class rules may change only racing rules 42, 49, 50, 51, 52, 53 and 54.

86.2    If a national authority so prescribes, these restrictions do not apply if rules are changed to develop or test proposed rules in local races. The national authority may prescribe that its approval is required for such changes.

87     **ORGANIZING AUTHORITY; NOTICE OF RACE;**       195
       **APPOINTMENT OF RACE OFFICIALS**

87.1    **Organizing Authority**

Races shall be organized by an organizing authority, which shall be

(a)   the ISAF;

(b)   a member national authority of the ISAF;

(c)   a club or other organization affiliated to a national authority;

(d)   a class association, either with the approval of a national authority or in conjunction with an affiliated club; or

(e)   an unaffiliated body in conjunction with an affiliated club, except that in a major event designated by the ISAF, the unaffiliated body shall be owned and controlled by an affiliated club which shall have the approval of the relevant national authority.

**87.2   Notice of Race; Appointment of Race Officials**
The organizing authority shall publish a notice of race that conforms to rule J1, appoint a race committee and, when appropriate, appoint a jury. However, the race committee, an international jury and umpires may be appointed by the ISAF as provided by the ISAF regulations.

**88      RACE COMMITTEE; SAILING INSTRUCTIONS; SCORING**

**88.1   Race Committee**
The race committee shall conduct races as directed by the organizing authority and as required by the *rules.*

**88.2   Sailing Instructions**

(a)   The race committee shall publish written sailing instructions that conform to rule J2.
(b)   The sailing instructions for an international event shall include, in English, the applicable prescriptions of the national authority.

(c)   Changes to the sailing instructions shall be in writing and posted within the required time on the official notice board or, on the water, communicated to each boat before her warning signal. Oral changes may be given only on the water, and only if the procedure is stated in the sailing instructions.

**88.3   Scoring**

(a)   The race committee shall score a race or series as provided in Appendix A using either the Low Point or Bonus Point system, or as otherwise specified in the sailing instructions.
(b)   When a scoring system provides for excluding one or more race scores from a boat's series score, the score for a breach of rule 2, rule 30.3's next-to-last sentence, or rule 42 if rule 67, N2.2 or N2.3 applies, shall not be excluded. The next-worse score shall be excluded instead.

89    **PROTEST COMMITTEE**                                    page
      A protest committee shall be

      (a)   a committee appointed by the race committee;
      (b)   a jury appointed by the organizing authority, which is
            separate from and independent of the race committee;
            or
      (c)   an international jury appointed by the organizing     *222*
            authority or as prescribed in the ISAF regulations and
            meeting the requirements of Appendix M. A national
            authority may prescribe that its approval is required for
            the appointment of international juries for races within
            its jurisdiction, except ISAF events or when internation-
            al juries are appointed by the ISAF under rule 87.2.

# APPENDICES, SECTION I

## APPENDIX A – SCORING

*See rule 88.3.*

**A1      NUMBER OF RACES**

The number of races scheduled and the number required to be completed to constitute a series shall be stated in the sailing instructions.

**A2      SERIES SCORES**

Each boat's series score shall be the total of her race scores excluding her worst score. (The sailing instructions may make a different arrangement by providing, for example, that no score will be excluded, that two or more scores will be excluded, or that a specified number of scores will be excluded if a specified number of races are completed.) If a boat has two or more equal worst scores, the score(s) for the race(s) sailed earliest in the series shall be excluded. The boat with the lowest series score wins and others shall be ranked accordingly.

**A3      STARTING TIMES AND FINISHING PLACES**

The time of a boat's starting signal shall be her starting time, and the order in which boats *finish* a race shall determine their finishing places. However, when a handicap system is used a boat's elapsed time, corrected to the nearest second, shall determine her finishing place.

**A4      LOW POINT AND BONUS POINT SYSTEMS**

Most series are scored using either the Low Point System or the Bonus Point System. The Low Point System uses a boat's *finishing* place as her race score. The Bonus Point System benefits the first six finishers because of the greater difficulty in advancing from fourth place to third, for example, than from fourteenth place to thirteenth. The system chosen may be made to apply by stating in the sailing instructions that, for example, 'The series will be scored as provided in Appendix A of the racing rules using the [Low] [Bonus] Point System.'

**A4.1**    Each boat *starting* and *finishing* and not thereafter retiring, being penalized or given redress shall be scored points as follows:

| Finishing place | Low Point System | Bonus Point System | page |
|---|---|---|---|
| First | 1 | 0 | |
| Second | 2 | 3 | |
| Third | 3 | 5·7 | |
| Fourth | 4 | 8 | |
| Fifth | 5 | 10 | |
| Sixth | 6 | 11·7 | |
| Seventh | 7 | 13 | |
| Each place thereafter | Add 1 point | Add 1 point | |

**A4.2** A boat that did not *start*, did not *finish*, retired after *finishing* or was disqualified shall be scored points for the finishing place one more than the number of boats entered in the series. A boat penalized under rule 30.2 or 44.3 shall be scored points as provided in rule 44.3(c).

**A5 SCORES DETERMINED BY THE RACE COMMITTEE**
A boat that did not *start*, comply with rule 30.2 or 30.3, or *finish*, or that takes a penalty under rule 44.3 or retires after *finishing*, shall be scored accordingly by the race committee without a hearing. Only the protest committee may take other scoring actions that worsen a boat's score.

**A6 CHANGES IN PLACES AND SCORES OF OTHER BOATS**

(a) If a boat is disqualified from a race or retires after *finishing*, each boat that *finished* after her shall be moved up one place.
(b) If the protest committee decides to give redress by adjusting a boat's score, the scores of other boats shall not be changed unless the protest committee decides otherwise.

**A7 RACE TIES**
If boats are tied at the finishing line or if a handicap system is used and boats have equal corrected times, the points for the place for which the boats have tied and for the place(s) immediately below shall be added together and divided equally. Boats tied for a race prize shall share it or be given equal prizes.

**A8    SERIES TIES**

A8.1    If there is a series score tie between two or more boats, each boat's race scores shall be listed in order of best to worst, and at the first point(s) where there is a difference the tie shall be broken in favour of the boat(s) with the best score(s). No excluded scores shall be used.

A8.2    If a tie remains between two boats, it shall be broken in favour of the boat that scored better than the other boat in more races. If more than two boats are tied, they shall be ranked in order of the number of times each boat scored better than another of the tied boats. No race for which a tied boat's score has been excluded shall be used.

A8.3    If a tie still remains between two or more boats, they shall be ranked in order of their scores in the last race. Any remaining ties shall be broken by using the tied boats' scores in the next-to-last race and so on until all ties are broken. These scores shall be used even if some of them are excluded scores.

**A9    RACE SCORES IN A SERIES LONGER THAN A REGATTA**
For a series that is held over a period of time longer than a regatta, a boat that came to the starting area but did not *start*, did not *finish*, retired after *finishing* or was disqualified shall be scored points for the finishing place one more than the number of boats that came to the starting area. A boat that did not come to the starting area shall be scored points for the finishing place one more than the number of boats entered in the series.

**A10    GUIDANCE ON REDRESS**
If the protest committee decides to give redress by adjusting a boat's score for a race, it is advised to consider scoring her

(a)    points equal to the average, to the nearest tenth of a point (0.05 to be rounded upward), of her points in all the races in the series except the race in question;

(b)    points equal to the average, to the nearest tenth of a point (0.05 to be rounded upward), of her points in all the races before the race in question; or

(c)    points based on the position of the boat in the race at the time of the incident that justified redress.

A11  **SCORING ABBREVIATIONS**                                   page
     These abbreviations are recommended for recording the cir-
     cumstances described:

DNC  Did not *start;* did not come to the starting area
DNS  Did not *start* (other than DNC and OCS)
OCS  Did not *start;* on the course side of the starting line and broke
     rule 29.1 or 30.1
ZFP  20% penalty under rule 30.2
BFD  Disqualification under rule 30.3
SCP  Took a scoring penalty under rule 44.3
DNF  Did not *finish*
RAF  Retired after *finishing*
DSQ  Disqualification
DNE  Disqualification not excludable under rule 88.3(b)
RDG  Redress given

# APPENDIX B – SAILBOARD RACING RULES

*Sailboard races shall be sailed under* The Racing Rules of Sailing *as changed by this appendix.*

B1   **DEFINITIONS**
     Add the following definitions:

     **Capsized**    A sailboard is *capsized* when her sail or the
                     competitor's body is in the water.

     **Recovering**  A sailboard is *recovering* from the time her sail
                     or, when water-starting, the competitor's body
                     is out of the water until she has steerage way.

B2   **PART 2 – WHEN BOATS MEET**

B2.1 The last sentence of rule 20 is changed to: 'A sailboard mov-
     ing astern shall *keep clear* of other sailboards and boats.'

**B2.2**   Add to Section D:

**23**   **Sail Out of the Water When Starting**
When approaching the starting line to *start*, a sailboard shall have her sail out of the water and in a normal position, except when accidentally *capsized*.

**24**   **Recovering**
A sailboard *recovering* shall avoid a sailboard or boat under way.

**B3**   **PART 3 – CONDUCT OF A RACE**
Rule 31 is changed to: 'A competitor shall not hold on to a starting *mark*.'

**B4**   **PART 4 – OTHER REQUIREMENTS WHEN RACING**

**B4.1**   Rule 42 is changed to: 'A sailboard shall be propelled only by the action of the wind on the sail, by the action of the water on the hull and by the unassisted actions of the competitor.'

**B4.2**   Rule 43.1(a) is modified to permit a competitor to wear a container for holding beverages. The container shall have a capacity of at least one litre and weigh no more than 1.5 kilograms when full.

**B4.3**   In rule 44.2, delete 'including two tacks and two gybes'.

**B5**   **PART 6 – ENTRY AND QUALIFICATION**
Add to rule 78.1: 'When so prescribed by the national authority, a numbered and dated device on a sailboard and her daggerboard and sail shall serve as her measurement certificate.'

**B6**   **PART 7 – RACE ORGANIZATION**
In rule 88.2(c), the last sentence is changed to: 'Changes to the sailing instructions may be communicated orally, but only if the procedure is stated in the sailing instructions.'

**B7**   **APPENDIX G – IDENTIFICATION ON SAILS**

**B7.1**   Add to rule G1.1(a): 'The insignia shall not refer to anything other than the manufacturer or class and shall not consist of more than two letters and three numbers or an abstract design.'

B7.2 Rules G1.3(a), G1.3(c), G1.3(d) and G1.3(e) are changed to: 'The class insignia shall be displayed once on each side of the sail in the area above a line projected at right angles from a point on the luff of the sail one third of the distance from the head to the wishbone. The national letters and sail numbers shall be in the central third of the sail above the wishbone and clearly separated from any advertising and shall be placed at different heights on the two sides of the sail, those on the starboard side being uppermost.'

# APPENDIX C – MATCH RACING RULES

*Match races shall be sailed under* The Racing Rules of Sailing *as changed by this appendix. Matches shall be umpired unless the notice of race and sailing instructions state otherwise.*

## C1 TERMINOLOGY
'Competitor' means the skipper, team or boat as appropriate for the event. 'Flight' means two or more matches started in the same starting sequence.

## C2 CHANGES TO THE DEFINITIONS AND THE RULES OF PART 2

C2.1 The definition *Finish* is changed to: 'A boat *finishes* when any part of her hull, crew or equipment in normal position, crosses the finishing line in the direction of the course from the last *mark* after completing any penalties. However, when penalties are cancelled under rule C7.2(d) after one or both boats have *finished* each shall be recorded as *finished* when she crossed the line.'

C2.2 Add to the definition *Proper Course*: 'A boat taking a penalty or manoeuvring to take a penalty is not sailing a *proper course*.'

C2.3 Change the last sentence of the definition *Clear Ahead* and *Clear Astern; Overlap* to: 'These terms do not apply to boats on opposite tacks unless either rule 18 applies or both boats are subject to rule 13.2.'

**C2.4**    Rule 13 becomes rule 13.1.

Add new rule 13.2: 'After the foot of the mainsail of a boat sailing downwind crosses the centreline she shall *keep clear* until her mainsail has filled on the other *tack.*'

**C2.5**    Rules 16.2 and 17.2 are deleted.

**C2.6**    Rule 18.3 is changed to: 'If two boats were on opposite *tacks* and one of them completes a tack within the *two-length zone* to pass a *mark* or *obstruction,* and if thereafter the other boat cannot by luffing avoid becoming *overlapped* inside her, the boat that tacked shall *keep clear* and rules 15 and 18.2 do not apply. If the other boat can by luffing avoid becoming *overlapped* inside her then rule 18.2(c) shall apply as if the boats were *clear ahead* and *clear astern* at the *two-length zone.*'

**C2.7**    When rule 19.1 applies, the following arm signals by the helmsman are required in addition to the hails:

(a)   for 'Room to tack', repeatedly and clearly pointing to windward; and

(b)   for 'You tack', repeatedly and clearly pointing at the other boat and waving the arm to windward.

**C2.8**    In rule 20 the second sentence is changed to: 'A boat taking a penalty shall *keep clear* of one that is not.'

**C2.9**    Rule 22.1 is changed to: 'If reasonably possible, a boat not *racing* shall not interfere with a boat that is *racing* or an umpire boat.'

**C2.10**   Rule 22.2 is changed to: 'Except when sailing a *proper course,* a boat shall not interfere with a boat taking a penalty or sailing on another leg.'

**C2.11**   Add new rule 22.3: 'When boats in different matches meet, any change of course by either boat shall be consistent with complying with a *rule* or trying to win her own match.'

**C3**      **RACE SIGNALS AND CHANGES TO RELATED RULES**

**C3.1**    **Starting Signals**
The signals for starting a match shall be as follows. Times shall be taken from the visual signals; the failure of a sound signal shall be disregarded. If more than one match will be sailed, the

starting signal for one match shall be the warning signal for the next match.

| Time in minutes | Visual signal | Sound signal | Means |
|---|---|---|---|
| 10 | Flag F displayed | One | Attention |
| 6 | Flag F removed | None | |
| 5 | Numeral pennant displayed* | One | Warning signal |
| 4 | Flag P displayed | One | Preparatory signal |
| 2 | Blue or yellow flag or both displayed** | One** | End of pre-start entry time |
| 0 | Warning and preparatory signals removed | One | Starting signal |

*Within a flight, numeral pennant 1 means Match 1, pennant 2 means Match 2, etc., unless the sailing instructions state otherwise.

**These signals shall be made only if one or both boats fail to comply with rule C4.2. The flag(s) shall be displayed until the umpires have signalled a penalty or for one minute, whichever is earlier.

## C3.2  Changes to Related Rules

(a) Rule 29.1 is changed to: 'When at a boat's starting signal any part of her hull, crew or equipment is on the course side of the starting line or its extensions, she shall sail completely on the pre-start side of the line before *starting*.'

(b) Rule 29.2 is changed to: 'When at her starting signal a boat becomes subject to rule C3.2(a), the race committee shall promptly display a blue or yellow flag or both with one sound signal. Each flag shall be displayed until such boats are completely on the pre-start side of the starting line or its extensions or until two minutes after her starting signal, whichever is earlier.'

(c) When, after her starting signal, a boat sails on the course side of the starting line or its extensions, without having started correctly, the race committee shall promptly display a blue or yellow flag or both. Each flag shall be displayed until such boats are completely on the pre-start side of the starting line or its extensions or until two minutes after her starting signal, whichever is earlier.

    (d)   In Race Signal AP the last sentence is changed to: 'The attention signal will be made 1 minute after removal unless at that time the race is *postponed* again or *abandoned.*'

    (e)   In Race Signal N the last sentence is changed to: 'The attention signal will be made 1 minute after removal unless at that time the race is *abandoned* again or *postponed.*'

**C3.3**   **Finishing Line Signals**

The race signal 'Blue flag or shape' shall not be used.

**C4**   **REQUIREMENTS BEFORE THE START**

**C4.1**   At her preparatory signal, each boat shall be outside the line that is at 90° angle to the starting line through the starting *mark* at her assigned end. In the race schedule pairing list, the boat listed on the left-hand side is assigned the port end and shall display a blue flag at her stern while *racing.* The other boat is assigned the starboard end and shall display a yellow flag at her stern while *racing.*

**C4.2**   Within the two-minute period following her preparatory signal, a boat shall cross and clear the starting line, the first time from the course side to the pre-start side.

**C5**   **SIGNALS BY UMPIRES**

    (a)   A green and white flag with one long sound signal means: 'No penalty.'

    (b)   A coloured flag identifying a boat with one long sound signal means: 'The identified boat shall take a penalty by complying with rule C7.'

    (c)   A red flag with or soon after a coloured flag with one long sound signal means: 'The identified boat shall take a penalty by complying with rule C7.3(d).'

    (d)   A black flag with a coloured flag and one long sound signal means: 'The identified boat is disqualified, and the match is terminated and awarded to the other boat.'

    (e)   One short sound signal means: 'A penalty is now completed.'

    (f)   Repetitive short sound signals mean: 'A boat is no longer taking a penalty and the penalty remains.'

    (g)   A coloured shape displayed from an umpire boat means: 'The identified boat has an outstanding penalty.'

| C6 | PROTESTS AND REQUESTS FOR REDRESS BY BOATS | page |

**C6.1**  A boat may protest another boat

   (a)  under a rule of Part 2, except rule 14, by clearly displaying flag Y immediately after an incident in which she was involved.

   (b)  under any rule not listed in rule C6.1(a) or C6.2 by clearly displaying a red flag as soon as possible after the incident.

**C6.2**  A boat may not protest another boat under

   (a)  rule 14, unless damage results;

   (b)  a rule of Part 2, unless she was involved in the incident;

   (c)  rule 31 or 42; or

   (d)  rule C4 or C7.

**C6.3**  A boat intending to request redress because of circumstances that arise before she *finishes* or retires shall clearly display a red flag as soon as possible after she becomes aware of those circumstances, but not later than two minutes after *finishing* or retiring.

**C6.4**  (a)  A boat protesting under rule C6.1(a) shall remove flag Y before or as soon as possible after the umpires' signal.

   (b)  A boat protesting under rule C6.1(b) or requesting redress under rule C6.3 shall, for her *protest* to be valid, keep her red flag displayed until she has so informed the umpires after *finishing* or retiring.

**C6.5**  **Umpire Decisions**
After flag Y is displayed, the umpires shall decide whether to penalize any boat. They shall signal their decision in compliance with rule C5(a), (b) or (c).

**C6.6**  **Protest Committee Decisions**

   (a)  The protest committee may take evidence in any way it considers appropriate and may communicate its decision orally.

   (b)  If the protest committee decides that a breach of a *rule* has had no significant effect on the outcome of the match, it may

      (1)  impose a penalty of one point or part of one point,

      (2)  order a resail, or

      (3)  make another arrangement it decides is equitable, which may be to impose no penalty.

(c)   The penalty for breaking rule 14 when damage results will be at the discretion of the protest committee, and may include exclusion from further races in the event.

## C7      PENALTY SYSTEM

### C7.1    Rule Changes
Rules 31.2 and 44 are deleted.

### C7.2    All Penalties
(a)   A penalized boat may delay taking a penalty within the limitations of rule C7.3 and shall take it as follows:

    (1)   When on a leg of the course to a windward *mark,* she shall gybe and, as soon as reasonably possible, luff to a close-hauled course.

    (2)   When on a leg of the course to a leeward *mark* or the finishing line, she shall tack and, as soon as reasonably possible, bear away to a downwind course.

(b)   Add to rule 2: 'When *racing,* a boat may wait for an umpire's decision before taking a penalty.'

(c)   A boat completes a leg of the course when her bow crosses the extension of the line from the previous *mark* through the *mark* she is rounding, or on the last leg when she *finishes.*

(d)   A penalized boat shall not be recorded as having *finished* until she takes her penalty and sails completely to the course side of the line and then *finishes,* unless the penalty is cancelled before or after she crosses the finishing line.

(e)   If a boat has one or two outstanding penalties and the other boat in her match is penalized, one penalty for each boat shall be cancelled except that a 'red flag' penalty shall not cancel an outstanding penalty.

(f)   If a boat has more than two outstanding penalties, the umpires shall signal her disqualification under rule C5(d).

### C7.3    Penalty Limitations

(a)   A boat taking a penalty that includes a tack shall have the spinnaker head below the main boom gooseneck from the time she passes head to wind until she is on a close-hauled course.

(b)   No part of a penalty may be taken within two of a boat's hull lengths of a rounding *mark.*

(c)   If a boat has one outstanding penalty, she may take the penalty any time after *starting* and before *finishing.* If a boat has two outstanding penalties, she shall take one of them as soon as reasonably possible, but not before *starting.*

(d) When the umpires display a red flag with or soon after a penalty flag, the penalized boat shall take a penalty as soon as reasonably possible, but not before *starting.* A 'red flag' penalty shall not cancel an outstanding penalty.

**C7.4 Taking and Completing Penalties**

(a) When a boat with an outstanding penalty is on a leg to a windward *mark* and gybes, or is on a leg to a leeward *mark* or the finishing line and passes head to wind, she is taking a penalty.

(b) When a boat taking a penalty either does not take the penalty correctly or does not complete the penalty as soon as reasonably possible, she is no longer taking a penalty. The umpires shall signal this as required by rule C5(f).

(c) The umpire boat for each match shall display coloured shapes, each shape indicating one outstanding penalty. When a boat has taken a penalty, or a penalty has been cancelled, one shape shall be removed. Failure of the umpires to display or remove shapes shall not change the number of penalties outstanding.

**C8 PENALTIES INITIATED BY UMPIRES**

**C8.1 Rule Changes**

(a) Rules 60.2(a) and 60.3(a) do not apply to *rules* for which penalties may be imposed by umpires.

(b) Rule 64.1(b) is changed so that the provision for exonerating a boat may be applied by the umpires without a hearing, and it takes precedence over any conflicting rule of this appendix.

**C8.2** When the umpires decide that a boat has broken rule 31, 42, C4 or C7.3(c) she shall be penalized by signalling her under rule C5(b).

**C8.3** When the umpires decide that a boat has

(a) gained an advantage by breaking a *rule* after allowing for a penalty,

(b) deliberately broken a *rule,* or

(c) committed a breach of sportsmanship,

she shall be penalized under rule C5(b) or C5(d).

**C8.4** If the umpires or protest committee members decide that a boat may have broken a *rule* other than those listed in rule C6.1(a) or C6.2, they shall so inform the protest committee for its action under rule 60.3 and rule C6.6 when appropriate.

**C8.5** When, after one boat has *started*, the umpires are satisfied that the other boat will not *start*, they may signal under rule C5(d) that the boat that did not *start* is disqualified and the match is terminated.

## C9 REQUESTS FOR REDRESS OR REOPENINGS, APPEALS, OTHER PROCEEDINGS

**C9.1** There shall be no request for redress or an appeal from a decision made under rule C5, C6, C7 or C8. In rule 66 the third sentence is changed to: 'A *party* to the hearing may not ask for a reopening.'

**C9.2** A competitor may not base a request for redress on a claim that an action by an official boat was improper. The protest committee may decide to consider giving redress in such circumstances but only if it believes that an official boat, including an umpire boat, may have seriously interfered with a competing boat.

**C9.3** No proceedings of any kind may be taken in relation to any action or non-action by the umpires, except as permitted in rule C9.2.

## C10 SCORING

**C10.1** The winning competitor of each match scores one point (half of one point each for a dead heat); the loser scores no points.

**C10.2** When a competitor withdraws from part of an event the scores of all completed races shall stand.

**C10.3** When a multiple round-robin is terminated with an incomplete round-robin, only one point shall be available for all the matches sailed between any two competitors, as follows:

| *Number of matches completed between any two competitors* | *Points for each win* |
| --- | --- |
| 1 | One point |
| 2 | One-half point |
| 3 | One-third point |
| (etc) | |

**C10.4** In a round-robin series,

(a) competitors shall be placed in order of their total scores, highest score first;

(b) a competitor who has won a match but is disqualified for breaking a *rule* against a competitor in another match shall lose the point for that match (but the losing competitor shall not be awarded the point); and

(c) the overall position between competitors who have sailed in different groups shall be decided by the highest score.

**C10.5** In a knockout series the sailing instructions shall prescribe the minimum number of points required to win a series between two competitors. When a knockout series is terminated it shall be decided in favour of the competitor with the higher score.

## C11   TIES

### C11.1   Round-Robin Series

A round-robin series means a grouping of competitors who all sail against each other one or more times. Each separate stage identified in the event format shall be a separate round-robin series irrespective of the number of times each competitor sails against each other competitor in that stage.

Ties between two or more competitors in a round-robin series shall be broken by the following methods, in order, until the tie is broken. When the tie is only partially broken, paragraphs (a) to (e) shall be reapplied to the remaining ties. The tie shall be decided in favour of the competitor(s) who

(a) placed in order, has the highest score in the matches between the tied competitors.

(b) when the tie is between two competitors in a multiple round-robin, has won the last match between the two competitors.

(c) has the most points against the competitor placed highest in the round-robin series or, if necessary, second highest, and so on until the tie is broken.

When two separate ties have to be resolved but the resolution of each depends upon resolving the other, the following principles shall be used in the C11.1(c) procedure:

(1) the higher place tie shall be resolved before the lower place tie, and

(2) all the competitors in the lower place tie shall be

treated as a single competitor for the purposes of rule C11.1(c).

(d) after applying rule C10.4(c), has the highest place in the different groups, irrespective of the number of competitors in each group.

(e) has the highest place in the most recent stage of the event (fleet race, round-robin, etc).

**C11.2  Knockout Series**

Ties (including 0–0) between two competitors in a knockout series shall be broken by the following methods, in order, until the tie is broken. The tie shall be decided in favour of the competitor who

(a) has the highest place in the most recent round-robin series, applying rule C11.1 if necessary.

(b) has won the most recent match in the event between the tied competitors.

**C11.3**  When rule C11.1 or C11.2 does not resolve the tie:

(a) If the tie needs to be resolved for a later stage of the event (or another event for which the event is a direct qualifier), the tie shall be broken by a sail-off when practicable. When the race committee decides a sail-off is not practicable the tie shall be broken by a draw.

(b) To decide the winner of an event, or the overall position between competitors eliminated in one round of a knockout series, a sail-off may be used (but not a draw).

(c) When a tie is not broken any monetary prizes or ranking points for tied places shall be added together and divided equally among the tied competitors.

*Note: A Standard Notice of Race and Standard Sailing Instructions for match racing are available from the ISAF.*

# APPENDIX D – TEAM RACING RULES

*Team races shall be sailed under* The Racing Rules of Sailing *as changed by this appendix. If umpires or observers will be used the sailing instructions shall so state.*

**D1     CHANGES TO THE RACING RULES**

**D1.1**     The following rules are changed, added or deleted:

(a)     Rule 17.2 is changed to: 'Except on a beat to windward, while a boat is less than two of her hull lengths from a *leeward* boat, she shall not sail below her *proper course* unless she gybes.'

(b)     Rule 18.4 is deleted.

(c)     Add to rule 22.2: 'Except when sailing a *proper course*, a boat shall not interfere with a boat on another leg or lap of the course. For the purpose of this rule, a boat that has *finished* is on a different leg from one that has not.'

(d)     Add new rule 22.3: 'When boats in different races meet, any change of course by either boat shall be consistent with complying with a *rule* or trying to win her own race.'

(e)     Add to rule 41: 'A boat that receives help from a team-mate does not break this rule.'

**D1.2**     The following additional rules apply:

(a)     There shall be no penalty for breaking a rule of Part 2 when the incident is between boats in the same team and there is no contact.

(b)     A boat damaged by a team-mate boat is not eligible for redress based on that damage.

**D2     INTENTION TO PROTEST; ACKNOWLEDGEMENT OF BREACHES OF RULES**

**D2.1     General**

(a)     A boat intending to protest shall hail the other boat immediately and promptly display a red flag

(b)     A boat that, while *racing*, may have broken a rule of Part 2, except rule 14 when the boat has caused damage, or rule D1 may take a penalty as provided by rules 44.1 and 44.2, except that only one turn is required. When an incident occurs at the finishing line or when an umpire's penalty is signalled at or beyond the finishing line, a boat shall not be recorded as having *finished* until she has completed her penalty and sailed completely to the course side of the line before *finishing*.

(c) When after displaying a red flag a boat is satisfied that the other boat has taken a penalty in compliance with rule D2.1(b) she shall remove her red flag.

(d) A boat that has displayed a red flag and then decides reasonably promptly that she, and not the other boat, was at fault shall immediately remove her flag, take a penalty in compliance with rule D2.1(b), and hail the other boat accordingly.

(e) The sailing instructions may state that rule D2.2(g) applies to all *protests*.

### D2.2 Umpired Races

Races to be umpired shall be identified either in the sailing instructions or by the display of flag U no later than the warning signal.

(a) When a boat protests under a rule of Part 2, except rule 14, or under rule D1, 31.1, 42 or 44, she is not entitled to a hearing. Instead, when the protested boat fails either to acknowledge breaking a *rule* or to take a penalty in compliance with rule D2.1(b), the protesting boat may display a yellow flag and request a decision by hailing 'Umpire'.

(b) An umpire shall signal a decision as follows:
   (1) A green flag or a green and white flag means 'No penalty imposed; incident closed'.
   (2) A red flag means 'One or more boats are penalized.' The umpire shall hail or signal to identify each boat to be penalized.

   The protesting boat shall then remove her flag.

(c) A boat penalized by an umpire's decision shall make two 360° turns (720°) in compliance with rule 44.2.

(d) When a boat commits a breach of sportsmanship or fails to take a penalty when required by an umpire, or when a boat or her team gains an advantage despite taking a penalty, an umpire may impose one or more 360° turn penalties by displaying a red flag and hailing her accordingly, or report the incident as provided in rule D2.2(e).

(e) When an incident involves reckless sailing, rule 14 when damage may have been caused, rule 28.1 or failure to comply with an umpire's decision, the umpire may report the incident to a protest committee which may further penalize the boat concerned. The umpire shall signal this intention by displaying a black flag and hailing appropriately.

(f) Rules 60.2 and 60.3 do not apply. The protest committee may call a hearing only on receipt of a report from an umpire as provided in rule D2.2(e) or under rule 69.

(g) *Protests* need not be in writing, and the protest committee may take evidence in any way it considers appropriate and may communicate its decision orally.

(h) There shall be no requests for redress or to reopen a hearing or appeals by a boat arising from decisions or actions or non-actions by the umpires. The protest committee may decide to consider giving redress when it believes that an official boat, including an umpire boat, may have seriously interfered with a competing boat.

### D2.3 Races with Observers

Observers may be appointed by the race committee to observe the racing and give opinions on incidents when requested. If so, rule D2.2 applies except that

(a) a boat need not request an opinion or accept one, in which case any *protest* shall comply with and be decided under the rules of Part 5 as changed by this appendix;

(b) an observer may display a yellow flag to signal that he has no opinion. If a boat then intends to protest she may do so by complying with the rules of Part 5 as changed by this appendix.

### D3 SCORING A RACE

**D3.1** (a) Each boat *finishing* a race, whether or not rules 28.1 and 29.1 have been complied with, shall be scored points equal to her finishing place. All other boats shall be scored points equal to the number of boats entitled to *race*.

(b) In addition, a boat's score shall be increased as follows:

| Rule broken | Penalty points |
| --- | --- |
| (1) rule 14 when the boat has caused damage, or rule 29.1 | 10 |
| (2) any other *rule* for which a penalty has not been taken | 6 |

However, a boat that breaks rule 28.1 and does not *finish* shall not have the penalty points in (2) above added to her score for this breach when it gained neither her nor her team any advantage. The protest committee may further increase a boat's score when she has broken a *rule* and as a result her team has gained an advantage.

(c) The team with the lowest total points wins. If there is a tie on points, the team having the combination of race scores that does not include a first place wins.

**D3.2** When all boats of one team have *finished* or retired, the race committee may stop the race. The other team's boats shall be scored the points they would have received had they *finished*.

**D3.3** When all the boats of a team fail to *start* in a race, each shall be scored points equal to the number of boats entitled to *race*, and the boats of the other team shall be scored as if they had *finished* in the best positions.

## D4   SCORING A SERIES

**D4.1** A team racing series shall consist of races or matches. A match shall consist of two races between the same two teams. The team with the lower total points for the race or the match wins.

**D4.2** When two or more teams are competing in a series consisting of races or matches, the series winner shall be the team winning the greatest number of races or matches. The other teams shall be ranked in order of number of wins. Tied matches shall count as half a win to each team.

**D4.3** When necessary, ties in a completed series shall be broken using, in order of precedence,

(a) the number of races or matches won when the tied teams met;
(b) the points scored when the tied teams met;
(c) if two teams remain tied, the last race between them;
(d) total points scored in all races against common opponents;
(e) a game of chance.

If a multiple tie is only partially resolved by one of these, then the remaining tie shall be broken by starting again at rule D4.3(a).

**D4.4** If a series is not completed, teams shall be ranked according to the results from completed rounds, and ties shall be broken initially using the results from races or matches between the tied teams in the incomplete round. If no round has been completed, teams shall be ranked in order of their race (or match) win-loss ratios. Thereafter, rule D4.3(a) to D4.3(e) shall be used to break ties.

page

**D5 BREAKDOWNS WHEN BOATS ARE SUPPLIED BY THE ORGANIZING AUTHORITY**

**D5.1** A supplied boat suffering a breakdown shall display a red flag as soon as practicable and, if possible, continue *racing.*

**D5.2** When the race committee decides that the boat's finishing position was made significantly worse, that the breakdown was not the fault of the crew, and that in the same circumstances a reasonably competent crew would not have been able to avoid the breakdown, it shall make as equitable a decision as possible, which may be to order the race to be resailed or, when the boat's finishing position was predictable, award her points for that position. In case of doubt about her position when she broke down, the doubt shall be resolved against her.

**D5.3** A breakdown caused by defective supplied equipment or a breach of a *rule* by an opponent shall not normally be determined to be the fault of the crew, but one caused by careless handling, capsizing or a breach by a boat of the same team shall be. Any doubt about the fault of the crew shall be resolved in the boat's favour.

# APPENDIX E – RADIO-CONTROLLED BOAT RACING RULES

*Races for radio-controlled boats shall be sailed under* The Racing Rules of Sailing *as changed by this appendix.*

**E1 TERMINOLOGY, RACE SIGNALS, DEFINITIONS AND FUNDAMENTAL RULES**

**E1.1 Terminology**
'Boat' means a boat that is radio-controlled by a competitor

who is not on board. For 'race' used as a noun outside this appendix and Appendix A read 'heat'. Within this appendix, a race consists of one or more heats, and is completed when the last heat in the race is finished. An 'event' consists of one or more races. A 'series' consists of a specified number of races or events.

## E1.2 Race Signals

Race Signals do not apply. All signals shall be given orally or by other sounds described in this appendix.

## E1.3 Definitions

(a)  Add to the definition *Interested Party* 'but not a competitor when acting as an observer'.

(b)  In the definition *Two-Length Zone* change '*Two*' to '*Four*'.

## E1.4 Personal Buoyancy

Rule 1.2 is replaced with 'When on board a rescue vessel, each competitor shall be responsible for wearing personal buoyancy adequate for the conditions.'

## E1.5 Aerials

Transmitter aerial extremities shall be adequately protected. When a protest committee finds that a competitor has broken this rule it shall either warn him and give him time to comply or penalize him.

## E2 PART 2 – WHEN BOATS MEET

Rule 21 is replaced with:

### Capsized or Entangled

If possible, a boat shall avoid a boat that is capsized or entangled, or has not regained control after capsizing or entanglement. A boat is capsized when her masthead is in the water. Two or more boats are entangled when lying together for a period of time so that no boat is capable of manoeuvring to break free of the other(s).

## E3 PART 3 – CONDUCT OF A RACE

## E3.1 Races with Observers

The race committee may appoint race observers, who may be competitors. They shall remain in the control area, while boats are *racing* and they shall hail and repeat the identity of boats that contact a *mark* or another boat. Such hails shall be made from the control area. Observers shall report all unresolved incidents to the race committee at the end of the heat.

**E3.2 Course Board**

Rule J2.1(3) does not apply. A course board showing the course and the limits of the control area and launching area(s) shall be located next to or within the control area with information clearly visible to competitors while *racing*.

**E3.3 Control and Launching Areas**

The control and launching area(s) shall be defined by the sailing instructions. Competitors *racing* shall remain in the control area while a heat is in progress, except that competitors may briefly go to and return from the launching area to perform functions permitted in rule E4.5. Competitors not *racing* shall remain outside the control and launching areas except when offering assistance under rule E4.2 or when acting as race observers.

**E3.4 Non-applicable Rules**

The second sentence of rule 25 and all of rule 33 do not apply.

**E3.5 Starting Races**

Rule 26 is replaced with:

'Audible signals for starting a heat shall be at one-minute intervals and shall be a warning signal, a preparatory signal and a starting signal. During the minute before the starting signal, verbal signals shall be made at ten-second intervals, and during the final ten seconds at one-second intervals. The start shall be at the beginning of the starting signal.'

**E3.6 Starting Penalties**

In rules 29.1 and 30 delete the word 'crew'. Throughout rule 30 oral announcements shall replace the display of flag signals.

**E3.7 Starting and Finishing Lines**

The starting and finishing lines shall be tangential to, and on the course side of, the starting and finishing *marks*.

**E3.8 Individual Recall**

Rule 29.2 is changed. Delete all after 'the race committee shall promptly' and replace with 'twice hail "Recall (sail numbers)"'.

**E3.9** **General Recall**
Rule 29.3 is changed. Delete all after 'the race committee may' and replace with 'twice hail "General recall" with two sound signals'. After the recalled start, the warning signal for a new start shall be made.

**E3.10** **Shortening or Abandoning after the Start**
In rule 32.1(b) delete 'foul weather' and replace with 'thunderstorms'. Rules 32.1(c) and 32.2 do not apply.

**E4** **PART 4 – OTHER REQUIREMENTS WHEN RACING**

**E4.1** **Non-applicable rules**
Rules 42.2(b), 42.2(c), 42.3(a), 42.3(c), 43, 47, 48, 49, 50, 52 and 54 do not apply.

**E4.2** **Outside Help**
Rule 41 is replaced with:

(a) A competitor shall not give tactical or strategic advice to a competitor who is *racing.*

(b) A competitor who is *racing* shall not receive outside help except:

(1) A boat that has gone ashore or aground outside the launching area, or become entangled with another boat or *mark,* may be freed and relaunched only with outside help from a rescue vessel crew.

(2) Competitors who are not *racing* and others may give outside help in the launching area as permitted by rule E4.5.

**E4.3** **Propulsion and Prohibited Actions**

(a) In rule 42.1 delete all after 'sails and hull'.

(b) In rule 42.2(a) delete all after 'releasing the sail'.

**E4.4** **Penalties for Breaking a Rule of Part 2**
Throughout rule 44 the penalty shall be one 360° turn, including one tack and one gybe.

**E4.5** **Launching and Relaunching**
Rule 45 is replaced with:

(a) Except between the preparatory and starting signals, boats scheduled to *race* in a heat may be launched, taken ashore or relaunched at any time during the heat.

(b)  Boats shall be launched or recovered only from within a launching area, except as provided by rule E4.2(b)(1).

(c)  While ashore or within a launching area, boats may be adjusted, drained of water, or repaired; have their sails changed or reefed; have entangled objects removed; or have radio equipment repaired or changed.

**E4.6    Person in Charge**
Rule 46 is changed. Delete 'have on board' and replace with 'be radio-controlled by'.

**E4.7    Moving Ballast**
Rule 51 is replaced with:

During an event and unless class rules specify otherwise,

(a)  ballast shall not be shifted, shipped or unshipped;

(b)  except for replacements of similar weight and position, no control equipment shall be shifted, shipped or unshipped;

(c)  the position of rig counterbalance weights may be adjusted; and

(d)  bilge water shall not be used to trim the boat, but may be removed at any time.

**E4.8    Radio**

(a)  A competitor shall not transmit radio signals that cause interference with the radio reception of other boats.

(b)  A competitor found to have broken rule E4.8(a) shall not *race* until he has proven compliance with rule E4.8(a).

**E4.9    Boat Out of Radio Control**
A competitor who loses radio control of his boat shall promptly hail and repeat 'Out of control (the boat's sail number)'. Such a boat shall be deemed to have retired and shall be considered an *obstruction.*

**E5    PART 5 – PROTESTS, REDRESS, HEARINGS, MISCONDUCT AND APPEALS**

**E5.1    Right to Protest and Request Redress**
Add to rule 60.1(a): 'A *protest* alleging a breach of a rule of Part 2, 3 or 4 shall be made only by a competitor within the control or launching area and by a boat scheduled to *race* in the heat in which the incident occurred.' After the words 'report by a competitor from another boat' in rules 60.2(a) and 60.3(a) add 'except when acting as an observer'.

**E5.2    Informing the Protestee**

In rule 61.1(a) delete all after the first sentence and replace with 'When her *protest* concerns an incident in the racing area that she is involved in or sees, she shall twice hail '(Her own sail number) "protest" (the sail number of the other boat).'

**E5.3    Protest Time Limit**

In rule 61.3 delete 'two hours' and replace with '15 minutes'. Add 'A protestor intending to submit a *protest* shall inform the race committee within five minutes of the end of the relevant heat.'

**E5.4    Accepting Responsibility**

A boat that acknowledges breaking a rule of Part 2, 3 or 4 before the *protest* is found to be valid may retire from the relevant heat without further penalty.

**E5.5    Redress**

(a)    Add to rule 62.1:
   (e)    radio interference, or
   (f)    an entanglement or grounding because of the action of a boat that was breaking a rule of Part 2 or of a vessel not *racing* that was required to *keep clear*.

(b)    The first sentence of rule 62.2 is changed to 'The request shall be made in writing within the time limit of rule E5.3.'

**E5.6    Right to Be Present**

In rule 63.3(a) delete 'shall have been on board' and replace with 'shall have been radio-controlling them'.

**E5.7    Taking Evidence and Finding Facts**

Add to rule 63.6: 'Evidence about an alleged breach of a rule of Part 2, 3 or 4 given by competitors shall be accepted only from a competitor who was within the control or launching area and whose boat was scheduled to *race* in the heat in which the incident occurred.'

**E5.8    Penalties and Exoneration**

Instead of disqualification as provided by rule 64.1(a), the penalty for breaking rule E3.3, E4.2(a) or E4.5 may be determined by the protest committee to be

(a)    exclusion from the next race,
(b)    disqualification from the next race, or

(c)   one or more penalty turns that must be taken immediately after the boat has started her next race.

In these cases rule 64.1(c) does not apply.

**E5.9   Decision on Redress**
Add to rule 64.2: 'If a boat given redress was damaged, she shall be given reasonable time, but not more than 30 minutes, to effect repairs before her next heat.'

**E5.10   Reopening a Hearing**
In rule 66 '24 hours' is changed to 'ten minutes'.

**E6     APPENDIX G – IDENTIFICATION ON SAILS**
Appendix G is changed as follows:

(a)   In rule G1 add 'RSD' after 'ISAF'.
(b)   Rule G1.1(c) is replaced by: 'a sail number, which shall be the last two digits of the boat registration number, allotted by the relevant issuing authority.' Where this is a single-digit number, a '0' shall be placed in front. Alternatively an owner may be allotted a personal sail number by the relevant issuing authority, the last two digits of which may be used on all his boats. Where this is a single-digit number, a '0' shall be placed in front.
(c)   In rule G1.2(b) delete 'and opposite' and add to the table:

|  | *Minimum height* | *Minimum space between letters and numerals or edge of sail* |
| --- | --- | --- |
| numbers on RC boats | 100 mm | 13 mm |
| letters on RC boats | 60 mm | 13 mm |

Maximum dimensions shall be the minimum plus 10 mm. The space between marks on opposite sides of the sail shall be 60–100 mm. If a sail is too small to use the specified dimensions, smaller letters and numbers may be used, with 13 mm as the absolute minimum spacing.

(d)   Rule G1.3(c) is replaced by: 'Sail numbers shall be placed above the national letters. There shall be space in front of the sail number for the prefix '1', which may be prescribed by the race committee in the event of a conflict between numbers.'
(e)   Rule G1.3(e) is replaced by: 'The sail number shall be displayed on both sides of the headsail.'

# APPENDIX F – APPEALS PROCEDURES

*See rule 70. A national authority may change this appendix by prescription but it shall not be changed by sailing instructions.*

**F1    NATIONAL AUTHORITY**

Appeals, requests by protest committees for confirmation or correction of decisions, and requests for the interpretation of *rules* shall be made to the national authority.

**F2    APPELLANT'S RESPONSIBILITIES**

**F2.1**    Within 15 days of receiving the protest committee's written decision or its decision not to reopen a hearing, the appellant shall send a dated appeal to the national authority with a copy of the protest committee's decision. The appeal shall state why the appellant believes the protest committee's interpretation of a *rule* or its procedures were incorrect.

**F2.2**    The appellant shall also send, with the appeal or as soon as possible thereafter, any of the following documents that are available to her:

(a)    the written *protest(s)* or request(s) for redress;

(b)    a diagram, prepared or endorsed by the protest committee, showing the positions and tracks of all boats involved, the course to the next *mark* and the required side, the force and direction of the wind, and, if relevant, the depth of water and direction and speed of any current;

(c)    the notice of race, the sailing instructions, any other conditions governing the event, and any changes to them;

(d)    any additional relevant documents; and

(e)    the names and addresses of all *parties* to the hearing and the protest committee chairman.

**F2.3**    A request from a protest committee for confirmation or correction of its decision shall include the decision and all relevant documents. A request for a *rule* interpretation shall include assumed facts.

**F3    NOTIFICATION AND RESPONSE OF THE PROTEST COMMITTEE**

Upon receipt of an appeal, the national authority shall send a copy of the appeal to the protest committee, asking the protest committee for the documents listed in rule F2.2 not supplied by the appellant, and the protest committee shall send the documents to the national authority.

**F4    NATIONAL AUTHORITY'S RESPONSIBILITIES**
The national authority shall send copies of the appeal and the protest committee's decision to the other *parties* to the hearing. It shall send to the appellant copies of documents not sent by the appellant. It shall send to any *party* to the hearing upon request any of the documents listed in rule F2.2.

**F5    ADDITIONAL INFORMATION**
The national authority shall accept the protest committee's finding of facts except when it decides they are inadequate, in which case it may require the protest committee to provide additional facts or other information, or to reopen the hearing and report any new finding of facts.

**F6    COMMENTS**
*Parties* to the hearing and the protest committee may send comments on the appeal to the national authority, provided they do so within 15 days of receiving the appeal. The national authority shall send such comments to all *parties* to the hearing and to the protest committee.

**F7    WITHDRAWING AN APPEAL**
An appellant may withdraw an appeal before it is decided by accepting the protest committee's decision.

# APPENDIX G – IDENTIFICATION OF SAILS

*See rule 77.*

**G1    ISAF INTERNATIONAL CLASS BOATS**

**G1.1    Identification**
Every boat of an ISAF International Class or Recognized Class shall carry on her mainsail and, as provided in rules G1.3(d)

and G1.3(e) for letters and numbers only, on her spinnaker and headsail

(a)  the insignia denoting her class;

(b)  at all international events, except when the boats are provided to all competitors, national letters denoting her national authority from the table below. For the purposes of this rule, international events are ISAF events, world and continental championships, and events described as international events in their notices of race and sailing instructions; and

(c)  a sail number of no more than four digits allotted by her national authority or, when so required by the class rules, by the international class association. The four-digit limitation does not apply to classes whose ISAF membership or recognition took effect before 1 April 1997. Alternatively, if permitted in the class rules, an owner may be allotted a personal sail number by the relevant issuing authority, which may be used on all his boats in that class.

Sails measured before 31 March 1999 shall comply with rule G1.1 or with the rules applicable at the time of measurement.

| Letters | National authority | Letters | National authority |
|---|---|---|---|
| ALG | Algeria | CHI | Chile |
| ASA | American Samoa | CHN | China |
| AND | Andorra | TPE | Chinese Taipei |
| ANG | Angola | COL | Columbia |
| ANT | Antigua | COK | Cook Islands |
| ARG | Argentina | CRO | Croatia |
| ARM | Armenia | CUB | Cuba |
| AUS | Australia | CYP | Cyprus |
| AUT | Austria | CZE | Czech Republic |
| BAH | Bahamas | DEN | Denmark |
| BRN | Bahrain | DOM | Dominican Republic |
| BAR | Barbados | ECU | Ecuador |
| BLR | Belarus | EGY | Egypt |
| BEL | Belgium | ESA | El Salvador |
| BER | Bermuda | EST | Estonia |
| BRA | Brazil | FIJ | Fiji |
| IVB | British Virgin Islands | FIN | Finland |
| BRU | Brunei Darussalam | FRA | France |
| BUL | Bulgaria | GAB | Gabon |
| CAN | Canada | GEO | Georgia |

| Letters | National authority | Letters | National authority | page |
|---------|-------------------|---------|-------------------|------|
| GER | Germany | NGR | Nigeria | |
| CAY | Grand Cayman | NOR | Norway | |
| GBR | Great Britain | PAK | Pakistan | |
| GRE | Greece | PNG | Papua New Guinea | |
| GRN | Grenada | PAR | Paraguay | |
| GUM | Guam | PER | Peru | |
| GUA | Guatemala | PHI | Philippines | |
| HKG | Hong Kong | POL | Poland | |
| HUN | Hungary | POR | Portugal | |
| ISL | Iceland | PUR | Puerto Rico | |
| IND | India | QAT | Qatar | |
| INA | Indonesia | ROM | Romania | |
| IRL | Ireland | RUS | Russia | |
| ISR | Israel | SMR | San Marino | |
| ITA | Italy | SEY | Seychelles | |
| JAM | Jamaica | SIN | Singapore | |
| JPN | Japan | SVK | Slovak Republic | |
| KAZ | Kazakhstan | SLO | Slovenia | |
| KEN | Kenya | RSA | South Africa | |
| KOR | Korea | ESP | Spain | |
| KUW | Kuwait | SRI | Sri Lanka | |
| KGZ | Kyrghyzstan | LCA | St Lucia | |
| LAT | Latvia | SUD | Sudan | |
| LIB | Lebanon | SWE | Sweden | |
| LBA | Libya | SUI | Switzerland | |
| LIE | Liechtenstein | TAH | Tahiti | |
| LTU | Lithuania | THA | Thailand | |
| LUX | Luxembourg | TRI | Trinidad & Tobago | |
| MAS | Malaysia | TUN | Tunisia | |
| MLT | Malta | TUR | Turkey | |
| MRI | Mauritius | UKR | Ukraine | |
| MEX | Mexico | UAE | United Arab Emirates | |
| FSM | Micronesia | USA | United States of | |
| MDA | Moldova | | America | |
| MON | Monaco | URU | Uruguay | |
| MAR | Morocco | ISV | US Virgin Islands | |
| MYA | Myanmar | UZB | Uzbekistan | |
| NAM | Namibia | VEN | Venezuela | |
| NED | The Netherlands | YUG | Yugoslavia | |
| AHO | Netherlands Antilles | ZIM | Zimbabwe | |
| NZL | New Zealand | | | |

# ISAF Rules

### G1.2    Specifications

(a)    National letters and sail numbers shall be in capital letters and Arabic numerals, clearly legible and of the same
colour. Commercially available typefaces giving the same
or better legibility than Helvetica are acceptable.

(b)    The sizes of characters and minimum space between
adjoining characters on the same and opposite sides of
the sail shall be related to the boat's overall length as
follows:

| Overall length | Minimum height | Minimum space between letters and numerals or edge of sail |
| --- | --- | --- |
| under 3.5 m | 230 mm | 45 mm |
| 3.5 m–8.5 m | 300 mm | 60 mm |
| 8.5 m–11 m | 375 mm | 75 mm |
| over 11 m | 450 mm | 90 mm |

### G1.3    Positioning

Class insignia, national letters and sail numbers shall be posi-
tioned as follows:

(a)    Except as provided in (d) and (e) below, class insignia,
national letters and sail numbers shall when possible be
wholly above an arc whose centre is the head point and
whose radius is 60% of the leech length. They shall be
placed at different heights on the two sides of the sail,
those on the starboard side being uppermost.

(b)    The class insignia shall be placed above the national letters. If the class insignia is of such a design that two of
them coincide when placed back to back on both sides
of the sail, they may be so placed.

(c)    National letters shall be placed above the sail number.

(d)    The national letters and sail number shall be displayed
on the front side of a spinnaker but may be placed on
both sides. They shall be displayed wholly below an arc
whose centre is the head point and whose radius is 40%
of the foot median and, when possible, wholly above an
arc whose radius is 60% of the foot median.

(e)    The national letters and sail number shall be displayed on
both sides of a headsail whose clew can extend behind the
mast 30% or more of the mainsail foot length. They shall

page

be displayed wholly below an arc whose centre is the head point and whose radius is half the luff length and, if possible, wholly above an arc whose radius is 75% of the luff length.

## G2  OTHER BOATS

Other boats shall comply with the rules of their national authority or class association in regard to the allotment, carrying and size of insignia, letters and numbers. Such rules shall, when practicable, conform to the above requirements.

## G3  CHARTERED OR LOANED BOATS

When so stated in the notice of race or sailing instructions, a boat chartered or loaned for an event may carry national letters or a sail number in contravention of her class rules.

## G4  WARNINGS AND PENALTIES

When a protest committee finds that a boat has broken a rule of this appendix it shall either warn her and give her time to comply or penalize her.

## G5  CHANGES BY CLASS RULES

ISAF classes may change the rules of this appendix provided the changes have first been approved by the ISAF.

# APPENDIX H – WEIGHING CLOTHING AND EQUIPMENT

*See Rule 43. This appendix shall not be changed by sailing instructions or prescriptions of national authorities.*

H1  Items of clothing and equipment to be weighed shall be arranged on a rack. After being saturated in water the items shall be allowed to drain freely for one minute before being weighed. The rack must allow the items to hang as they would hang from clothes hangers, so as to allow the water to drain freely. Pockets that have drain-holes that cannot be closed shall be empty, but pockets or items that can hold water shall be full.

H2  When the weight recorded exceeds the amount permitted, the competitor may rearrange the items on the rack and the measurer shall again soak and weigh them. This procedure may be repeated a second time if the weight still exceeds the amount permitted.

H3  A competitor wearing a dry-suit may choose an alternative means of weighing the items.

(a) The dry-suit and items of clothing and equipment that are worn outside the dry-suit shall be weighed as described above.

(b) Clothing worn underneath the dry-suit shall be weighed as worn while *racing*, without draining.

(c) The two weights shall be added together.

# APPENDIX J – NOTICE OF RACE AND SAILING INSTRUCTIONS

*See rules 87.2 and 88.2(a). The term 'race' includes a regatta or other series of races.*

## J1  NOTICE OF RACE CONTENTS

J1.1  The notice of race shall include the following information:

(1) the title, place and dates of the race and name of the organizing authority;

(2) that the race will be governed by the *rules* as defined in *The Racing Rules of Sailing*;

(3) a list of any other documents that will govern the event (for example, the *Equipment Rules of Sailing*, to the extent that they apply);

(4) the classes to race, conditions of entry and any restrictions on entries;

(5) the times of registration and warning signals for the practice race or first race, and succeeding races if known.

J1.2  The notice of race shall include any of the following that would help competitors decide whether to attend the event or that conveys other information they will need before the sailing instructions become available:

(1)  that advertising will be restricted to Category A (see Appendix 1) and other information related to Appendix 1;

(2)  that the ISAF Competitor Classification System (or some other competitor classification system) will apply;

(3)  the procedure for advance registration or entry, including fees and any closing dates;

(4)  an entry form, to be signed by the boat's owner or owner's representative, containing words such as 'I agree to be bound by *The Racing Rules of Sailing* and by all other *rules* that govern this event';

(5)  measurement procedures or requirements for measurement or rating certificates;

(6)  the time and place at which the sailing instructions will be available;

(7)  any changes to the racing rules (see rule 86);

(8)  any changes to class rules, referring specifically to each rule and stating the change;

(9)  the courses to be sailed;

(10) the penalty for breaking a rule of Part 2, other than the 720° Turns Penalty;

(11) denial of the right of appeal, subject to rule 70.4;

(12) the scoring system, including the number of races scheduled and the minimum number that must be completed to constitute a series;

(13) prizes.

## J2    SAILING INSTRUCTION CONTENTS

**J2.1**  The sailing instructions shall include the following information:

(1)  that the race will be governed by the *rules* as defined in *The Racing Rules of Sailing*;

(2)  a list of any other documents that will govern the event (for example, the *Equipment Rules of Sailing*, to the extent that they apply);

(3)  the schedule of races, the classes to race and times of warning signals for each class;

(4)  the course(s) to be sailed, or a list of *marks* from which the course will be selected and, if relevant, how courses will be signalled;

(5)  descriptions of *marks*, including starting and finishing *marks*, stating the order and side on which each is to be left and identifying all rounding *marks* (see rule 28.1);

(6)  descriptions of the starting and finishing lines, class flags and any special signals to be used;

(7)   the time limit, if any, for *finishing*;

(8)   the scoring system, included by reference to Appendix A, to class rules or other *rules* governing the event, or stated in full. State the number of races scheduled and the minimum number that must be completed to constitute a series.

J2.2   The sailing instructions shall include those of the following that will apply:

(1)   that advertising will be restricted to Category A (see Appendix 1) and other information related to Appendix 1;

(2)   that the ISAF Competitor Classification System (or some other competitor classification system) will apply;

(3)   replacement of the relevant rules of Part 2 with the *International Regulations for Preventing Collisions at Sea* or other government right-of-way rules, the time(s) or place(s) they will apply, and any night signals to be used by the race committee;

(4)   changes to the racing rules permitted by rule 86, referring specifically to each rule and stating the change;

(5)   that the prescriptions of the national authority will not apply;

(6)   if the prescriptions of the national authority will apply at an international event, a copy in English of the prescriptions;

(7)   changes to class rules, referring specifically to each rule and stating the change;

(8)   restrictions controlling changes to boats when supplied by the organizing authority;

(9)   the registration procedure;

(10)   measurement or inspection procedure;

(11)   location(s) of official notice board(s);

(12)   procedure for changing the sailing instructions;

(13)   safety requirements, such as requirements and signals for personal buoyancy, check-in at the starting area, and check-out and check-in ashore;

(14)   declaration requirements;

(15)   signals to be made ashore and location of signal station(s);

(16)   the racing area (a chart is recommended);

(17)   approximate course length and approximate length of windward legs;

(18)   the time limit, if any, for boats other than the first boat to *finish*;

(19)  time allowances;

(20)  the location of the starting area and any applicable restrictions;

(21)  any special procedures or signals for individual or general recalls;

(22)  boats identifying *mark* locations;

(23)  procedure for changes of course after the start and any special signals;

(24)  any special procedure for shortening the course or for *finishing* a shortened course;

(25)  restrictions on use of support boats, plastic pools, radios, etc; on hauling out; and on outside assistance provided to a boat that is not *racing*;

(26)  the penalty for breaking a rule of Part 2, other than the 720° Turns Penalty;

(27)  penalization without a hearing under rule 67 for breaking rule 42;

(28)  whether Appendix N will apply;

(29)  protest procedure and times and place of hearings;

(30)  if rule M1.4(b) will apply, the time limit for requesting a hearing under that rule;

(31)  denial of the right of appeal, subject to rule 70.4;

(32)  the national authority's approval of the appointment of an international jury under rule 89(c);

(33)  substitution of competitors;

(34)  the minimum number of boats appearing in the starting area required for a race to be started;

(35)  when and where races *postponed* or *abandoned* for the day will be resailed;

(36)  tides and currents;

(37)  prizes;

(38)  other commitments of the race committee and obligations of boats.

# APPENDIX K – SAILING INSTRUCTIONS GUIDE

*This guide provides a set of tested sailing instructions designed primarily for major championship regattas for one or more classes. It therefore will be particularly useful for world, continental and national championships and other events of similar importance. The guide can also be useful for other events; however, for such events some of these instructions will be unnecessary or undesirable. Race officers should therefore be careful in making their choices.*

*An expanded version of the guide will be available on the ISAF website (www.sailing.org) and will contain provisions applicable to the largest and most complicated multi-class events, as well as variations on several of the sailing instructions recommended in this appendix. It will be revised from time to time, to reflect advances in race management techniques as they develop, and can be downloaded as a basic text for producing the sailing instructions for any particular event.*

*The principles on which all sailing instructions should be based are as follows:*

1    *They should include only two types of statement: the intentions of the race committee and the obligations of competitors.*
2    *They should be concerned only with racing. Information about social events, assignment of moorings, etc should be provided separately.*
3    *They should not change the racing rules except when clearly desirable.*
4    *They should not repeat or restate any of the racing rules.*
5    *They should not repeat themselves.*
6    *They should be in chronological order; that is, the order in which the competitor will use them.*
7    *They should, when possible, use words or phrases from the racing rules.*

*To use this guide, first review rule J2 and decide which instructions
will be needed. Instructions that are required by rule J2.1 are marked
with an asterisk (\*). Delete all inapplicable or unnecessary instructions. Select the version preferred where there is a choice. Follow the
directions in the left margin to fill in the spaces where a solid line
(⎯⎯⎯) appears and select the preferred wording if a choice or option
is shown in brackets ([ . . . ]).*

page

*After deleting unused instructions, renumber all instructions in
sequential order. Be sure that instruction numbers are correct
where one instruction refers to another.*

*On separate lines,
insert the full name
of the regatta, the
inclusive dates from
measurement or the
practice race until
the final race or clos-
ing ceremony, the
name of the organiz-
ing authority, and
the city and country.*

⎯⎯⎯⎯⎯⎯⎯⎯⎯⎯⎯⎯⎯⎯⎯⎯

⎯⎯⎯⎯⎯⎯⎯⎯⎯⎯⎯⎯⎯⎯⎯⎯

⎯⎯⎯⎯⎯⎯⎯⎯⎯⎯⎯⎯⎯⎯⎯⎯

⎯⎯⎯⎯⎯⎯⎯⎯⎯⎯⎯⎯⎯⎯⎯⎯

### SAILING INSTRUCTIONS

### 1   RULES

**1.1\*** The regatta will be governed by the 'rules' as
defined in the Racing Rules of Sailing.

*List by name any
other documents that
govern the event: for
example, the
Equipment Rules of
Sailing, to the extent
that they apply.*

**1.2\*** ⎯⎯⎯ will apply.

*Include only if the
prescriptions will not
apply. Insert the
name.*

**1.3** The prescriptions of the ⎯⎯⎯ national authority will not apply.

*Insert the rule
number(s) and class
name. Make a sepa-
rate statement for
the rules of each
class.*

**1.4** Rule(s) ⎯⎯⎯ of the ⎯⎯⎯ class rules [will not
apply] [is (are) changed as follows: ⎯⎯⎯].

**1.5** If there is a conflict between languages the English text will prevail.

## 2   NOTICES TO COMPETITORS

*Insert the location(s).*

Notices to competitors will be posted on the official notice board(s) located at _____.

## 3   CHANGES TO SAILING INSTRUCTIONS

*Change the times if different.*

Any change to the sailing instructions will be posted before 0900 on the day it will take effect, except that any change to the schedule of races will be posted by 2000 on the day before it will take effect.

## 4   SIGNALS MADE ASHORE

*Insert the location.*

**4.1** Signals made ashore will be displayed at _____.

*Insert the number of minutes.*

**4.2** When flag AP is displayed ashore, '1 minute' is replaced with 'not less than _____ minutes' in race signal AP.

**(OR)**

**4.2** Flag D with a sound signal means 'The warning signal will be made not less than _____ minutes after flag D is displayed. [Boats are requested not to leave the harbour until this signal is made.]'

*Delete if a class rule applies.*

**4.3** When flag Y is displayed ashore, rule 40 applies at all times while afloat. This changes the Part 4 preamble.

## 5   SCHEDULE OF RACES

*Revise as desired and insert the dates.*

**5.1\*** Racing is scheduled as follows:

| Date | Class ____ | Class ____ |
|------|-----------|-----------|
| _____ | racing | racing |
| _____ | racing | reserve day |
| _____ | reserve day | racing |
| _____ | racing | racing |
| _____ | racing | racing |

| | | | |
|---|---|---|---|
| *Insert the classes and numbers.* | **5.2\*** The numbers of races scheduled is as follows: | | page |

| Class | Number of races | Races per day |
|---|---|---|
| ____ | ____ | ____ |
| ____ | ____ | ____ |

(a) Reserve days may be used if races are not completed as scheduled or if the race committee considers it unlikely that races will be completed as scheduled.

(b) One extra race per day may be sailed, provided that no class becomes more than one race ahead of schedule.

*Insert the time.*

**5.3\*** The scheduled time of the warning signal for the first race each day is _____.

**5.4** When more than one race (or sequence of races, for two or more classes) will be held on the same day, the warning signal for each succeeding race will be made as soon as practicable. To alert boats that another race or sequence of races will begin soon, the postponement signal will be displayed for at least four minutes before a warning signal is displayed.

*Insert the time.*

**5.5** On the last day of the regatta no warning signal will be made after _____.

## 6    CLASS FLAGS

*Insert the classes and names or descriptions of the flags.*

Class flags will be:

| Class | Flag |
|---|---|
| ____ | ____ |
| ____ | ____ |
| ____ | ____ |

## 7    RACING AREAS

*Insert a number or letter.*

Attachment _____ shows the location of racing areas.

## 8   THE COURSES

*Insert a number or letter.
A method of illustrating various courses is shown in Addendum A.*

**8.1\*** The diagrams in Attachment _____ show the courses, including the approximate angles between legs, the order in which marks are to be passed, and the side on which each mark is to be left. [The approximate course length will be _____ .]

*Insert either 'Mark _____' with the number of the leeward mark or 'the midpoint of the starting line'.*

**8.2** No later than the warning signal, the race committee signal boat will display the approximate compass bearing from _____ to Mark 1.

**8.3** When there is a gate, boats shall sail between the gate marks from the direction of the previous mark and round either gate mark.

**8.4** Courses will not be shortened. This changes rule 32.

## 9   MARKS

*Change the mark numbers as needed and insert the descriptions of the marks. Use the second alternative when Marks 4S and 4P form a gate, with Mark 4S to be left to starboard and Mark 4P to port.*

**9.1\*** Marks 1, 2, 3 and 4 will be _____.

**(OR)**

**9.1\*** Marks 1, 2, 3, 4S and 4P will be _____.

*Insert the descriptions of the marks.*

**9.2** New marks, as provided in instruction 11.1, will be _____.

*Describe the starting and finishing marks: for example, the race committee signal boat at the starboard end and a buoy at the port end. Instruction 10.2 will describe the starting line and instruction 12.1 the finishing line.*

**9.3\*** The starting and finishing marks will be _____.

page

**9.4** A race committee boat signalling a change of course is a mark as provided in instruction 11.3.

## 10 THE START

*Include only if the asterisked option in rule 26 will be used. Insert the number of minutes.*

**10.1** Races will be started by using rule 26 with the warning signal given _____ minutes before the starting signal.

**(OR)**

*Describe any starting system other than that stated in rule 26.*

**10.1** Races will be started as follows: _____.

**10.2\*** The starting line will be between staffs displaying orange flags on the starting marks.

**(OR)**

**10.2\*** The starting line will be between a staff displaying an orange flag on the starting mark at the starboard end and the port-end starting mark.

**(OR)**

*Insert the description.*

**10.2\*** The starting line will be _____.

**10.3** Boats whose warning signal has not been made shall avoid the starting area.

*Insert the number of minutes.*

**10.4** A boat starting later than _____ minutes after her starting signal will be scored Did Not Start. This changes rule A4.1.

## 11 CHANGE OF THE POSITION OF THE NEXT MARK

**11.1** To change the position of the next mark, the race committee will move the original mark (or the finishing line) to a new position. The change will be signalled before the leading boat has begun the leg, although the mark may not yet be in the new position. Any mark to be rounded after rounding the moved mark may be relocated without further signalling to maintain the course configuration.

**(OR)**

**11.1** To change the position of the next mark, the race committee will lay a new mark (or move the finishing line) and remove the original mark as soon as practicable. The change will be signalled before the leading boat has begun the leg, although the new mark may not yet be in position. Any mark to be rounded after rounding the new mark may be relocated without further signalling to maintain the course configuration. When in a subsequent change a new mark is replaced, it will be replaced by an original mark.

*Insert the class(es).* **11.2** For the _____ class(es), rule 33 is changed so that, instead of displaying a compass bearing, the race committee will display a green [triangular] [board] [flag] if the direction is changed to starboard or a red [rectangular] [board] [flag] if the direction is changed to port.

*Reverse 'port' and 'starboard' when the mark is to be left to starboard.* **11.3** Except at a gate, boats shall pass between the race committee boat signalling the change of course and the nearby mark, leaving the mark to port and the race committee boat to starboard. This changes rule 28.1.

## 12    THE FINISH

**12.1\*** The finishing line will be between staffs displaying orange flags on the finishing marks.

**(OR)**

**12.1\*** The finishing line will be between a staff displaying an orange flag on the finishing mark at the starboard end and the port-end finishing mark.

**(OR)**

*Insert the description.* **12.1\*** The finishing line will be _____.

**12.2** When the course is shortened at a gate, a race committee boat near the gate will display flag S and boats shall finish by sailing through the gate from the direction of the previous mark.

# Appendix K

The finishing line will be between the gate marks. This changes race signal S.

## 13 PENALTY SYSTEM

*Include instruction 13.1 only when the 720° Turns Penalty will not be used. Insert the number of places or describe the penalties.*

**13.1** The Scoring Penalty, rule 44.3, will apply. The penalty will be _____ places.

**(OR)**

**13.1** The penalties are as follows: _____.

*Insert the class(es).*

**13.2** For the _____ class(es) rule 44.2 is changed so that the 720° turn is replaced by a 360° turn.

**13.3** A boat that has taken a penalty or retired under rule 31.2 or 44.1 shall complete an acknowledgement form at the race office within the protest time limit.

**13.4** As provided in rule 67, the [protest committee] [jury] may, without a hearing, penalize a boat that has broken rule 42.

**(OR)**

**13.4** Appendix N will apply [as changed by instruction 13.2].

## 14 TIME LIMITS

*Insert the classes and times. Omit the Mark 1 time limit if inapplicable.*

**14.1*** Time limits are as follows:

| Class | Time limit | Mark 1 time limit |
|---|---|---|
| ___ | ___ | ___ |
| ___ | ___ | ___ |
| ___ | ___ | ___ |

If no boat has passed Mark 1 within the Mark 1 time limit the race will be abandoned.

*Insert the time (or different times for different classes).*

**14.2** Boats failing to finish within _____ after the first boat sails the course and finishes will be scored Did Not Finish. This changes rules 35 and A4.1.

93

### 15    PROTESTS AND REQUESTS FOR REDRESS

**15.1** Protest forms are available at the race office. Protests shall be delivered there within the protest time limit.

*Change the time if different.*

**15.2** For each class, the protest time limit is 90 minutes after the last boat has finished the last race of the day. [The same protest time limit applies to all protests by the race committee and [protest committee] [jury] and to requests for redress. This changes rules 61.3 and 62.2.]

*Change the time if different.*
*Insert the location and time.*

**15.3** Notices will be posted within 30 minutes of the protest time limit to inform competitors of hearings in which they are parties or named as witnesses. Hearings will be held in the [jury office] beginning at _____.

**15.4** Notices of protests by the race committee or [protest committee] [jury] will be posted to inform boats under rule 61.1(b).

**15.5** A list of boats that, under instruction 13.4, have acknowledged breaking rule 42 or have been disqualified by the [protest committee] [jury] will be posted before the protest time limit.

**15.6** For the purpose of rule 64.3(b) the 'authority responsible' is the measurer appointed by the organizing authority.

**15.7** Breaches of instructions 10.3, 13.3, 17, 18.2, 21, 22 and 23 will not be grounds for a protest by a boat. This changes rule 60.1(a). Penalties for these breaches may be less than disqualification if the [protest committee] [jury] so decides.

**15.8** On the last day of the regatta a request for reopening a hearing shall be delivered

(a)   within the protest time limit if the party requesting reopening was informed of the decision on the previous day;

*Change the time if different.*

(b) no later than 30 minutes after the party requesting reopening was informed of the decision on that day.

This changes rule 66.

*Include if the protest committee is an international jury or another provision of rule 70.4 applies.*

15.9 Decisions of the jury will be final as provided in rule 70.4.

## 16 SCORING

16.1* The [Low Point] [Bonus Point] scoring system of Appendix A will apply.

**(OR)**

*Describe the system.*

16.1* The scoring system is as follows: _____.

*Insert the number.*

16.2* _____ races are required to be completed to constitute a series.

*Insert the numbers throughout.*

16.3 (a) When fewer than _____ races have been completed, a boat's series score will be the total of her race scores.

(b) When from _____ to _____ races have been completed, a boat's series score will be the total of her race scores excluding her worst score.

(c) When _____ or more races have been completed, a boat's series score will be the total of her race scores excluding her two worst scores.

## 17 SAFETY REGULATIONS

*Insert the procedure for check-in and check-out.*

17.1 Check-in and check-out: _____.

17.2 A boat that retires from a race shall notify the race committee as soon as possible.

## 18 REPLACEMENT OF CREW OR EQUIPMENT

18.1 Substitution of competitors will not be allowed without prior written approval of the [race committee] [protest committee] [jury].

page

**95**

**18.2** Substitution of damaged or lost equipment will not be allowed unless approved by the race committee. Requests for substitution shall be made to the committee at the first reasonable opportunity.

## 19 EQUIPMENT AND MEASUREMENT CHECKS

A boat or equipment may be inspected at any time for compliance with the class rules and sailing instructions. On the water, a boat can be instructed by a race committee measurer to proceed immediately to a designated area for inspection.

## 20 OFFICIAL BOATS

*Insert the descriptions. If appropriate, use different identification markings for boats performing different duties.*

Official boats will be marked as follows: _____.

## 21 SUPPORT BOATS

**21.1** Team leaders, coaches and other support personnel shall stay outside areas where boats are racing from the time of the preparatory signal for the first class to start until all boats have finished or the race committee signals a postponement, general recall or abandonment.

*Insert the identification markings. National flags are suitable at international events.*

**21.2** Support boats shall be marked with _____.

## 22 HAUL-OUT RESTRICTIONS

Keel boats shall not be hauled out during the regatta except with and according to the terms of prior written permission of the race committee.

## 23 DIVING EQUIPMENT AND PLASTIC POOLS

Underwater breathing apparatus and plastic pools or their equivalent shall not be used

around keel boats between the starting signal | page
of the first race and the end of the regatta.

## 24 RADIO COMMUNICATION

A boat shall neither make radio transmissions while racing nor receive radio communications not available to all boats. This restriction also applies to mobile telephones.

## 25 PRIZES

*When perpetual trophies will be awarded state their complete names.*

Prizes will be given as follows: _____.

## 26 DISCLAIMER OF LIABILITY

Competitors participate in the regatta entirely at their own risk. See rule 4, Decision to Race. The organizing authority will not accept any liability for material damage or personal injury or death sustained in conjunction with or prior to, during, or after the regatta.

## 27 INSURANCE

*Insert the currency and amount.*

Each participating boat shall be insured with valid third-party liability insurance with a minimum cover of _____ per event or the equivalent.

## Addendum A – Illustrating the Course

*Shown here are examples of course illustrations. Any course can be similarly shown. When there is more than one course, prepare a separate diagram for each course and state how each will be signalled.*

### A WINDWARD-LEEWARD COURSE

Start – 1 – 2 – 1 – 2 – Finish

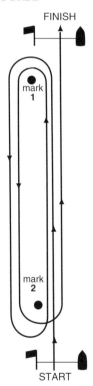

*Options for use with this course include*

(1)  *increasing or decreasing the number of laps,*

(2)  *deleting the final windward leg,*

(3)  *using a gate instead of a leeward **mark**,*

(4)  *using an offset **mark** at the windward **mark**, and*

(5)  *using the leeward and windward **marks** as starting and finishing **marks**.*

# A WINDWARD-LEEWARD-TRIANGLE COURSE

## Start – 1 – 2 – 3 – 1 – 3 – Finish

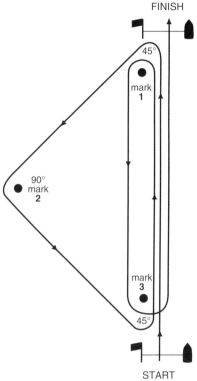

*Options for use with this course include*

*(1)   varying the interior angles of the triangle (45°–90°–45° and 60°–60°–60° are common),*

*(2)   deleting the last windward leg,*

*(3)   using a gate instead of a leeward **mark** for downwind legs (but not reaches),*

*(4)   using an offset **mark** at the beginning of downwind legs (but not reaches), and*

*(5)   using the leeward and windward **marks** as starting and finishing **marks**.*

*Be sure to specify the interior angle at each **mark**.*

## TRAPEZOID COURSES

Start – 1 – 2 – 3 – 2 – 3 – Finish

Start – 1 – 4 – 1 – 2 – 3 – Finish

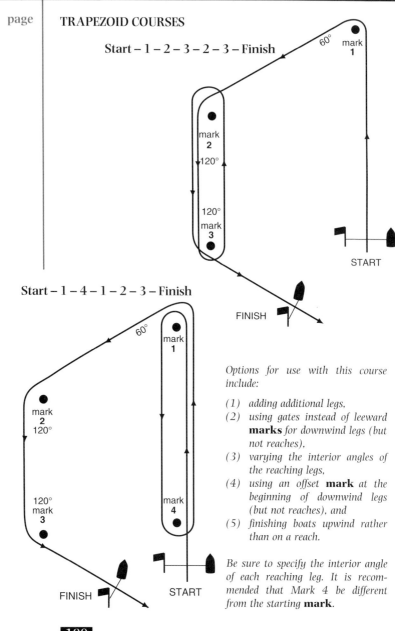

*Options for use with this course
include:*

*(1) adding additional legs,*

*(2) using gates instead of leeward
**marks** for downwind legs (but
not reaches),*

*(3) varying the interior angles of
the reaching legs,*

*(4) using an offset **mark** at the
beginning of downwind legs
(but not reaches), and*

*(5) finishing boats upwind rather
than on a reach.*

*Be sure to specify the interior angle
of each reaching leg. It is recommended that Mark 4 be different
from the starting **mark**.*

## Addendum B – Boats Provided by the Organizing Authority

*The following sailing instruction is recommended when all boats will be provided by the organizing authority. It can be changed to suit the circumstances. When used, it should be inserted after instruction 3.*

**4**      **BOATS**

**4.1**      Boats will be provided for all competitors, who shall not modify them or cause them to be modified in any way except that

(a)      a compass may be tied or taped to the hull or spars;

(b)      wind indicators, including yarn or thread, may be tied or taped anywhere on the boat;

(c)      hulls, centreboards and rudders may be cleaned, but only with water;

(d)      adhesive tape may be used anywhere above the water line; and

(e)      all fittings or equipment designed to be adjusted may be adjusted, provided that the class rules are complied with.

**4.2**      All equipment provided with the boat for sailing purposes shall be in the boat while afloat.

**4.3**      The penalty for not complying with one of the above instructions will be disqualification from all races sailed in which the instruction was broken.

**4.4**      Competitors shall report any damage or loss of equipment, however slight, to the organizing authority's representative immediately after securing the boat ashore. The penalty for breaking this instruction, unless the [jury] [protest committee] is satisfied that the competitor made a determined effort to comply, will be disqualification from the race most recently sailed.

**4.5**      Class rules requiring competitors to be members of the class association will not apply.

# APPENDIX L – RECOMMENDATIONS FOR PROTEST COMMITTEES

*This appendix is advisory only; in some circumstances changing these procedures may be advisable. It is addressed primarily to protest committee chairmen but may also help judges, jury secretaries, race committees and others connected with protest and redress hearings.*

In a *protest* or redress hearing, the protest committee should weigh all testimony with equal care; should recognize that honest testimony can vary, and even be in conflict, as a result of different observations and recollections; should resolve such differences as best it can; should recognize that no boat or competitor is guilty until a breach of a *rule* has been established to the satisfaction of the protest committee; and should keep an open mind until all the evidence has been heard as to whether a boat or competitor has broken a *rule*.

## L1 PRELIMINARIES (may be performed by race office staff)

- Receive the *protest* or request for redress.
- Note on the form the time the *protest* or request is delivered and the protest time limit.
- Inform each *party*, and the race committee when necessary, when and where the hearing will be held.

## L2 BEFORE THE HEARING
Make sure that

- each *party* has a copy of the *protest* or request for redress. When copies are unavailable let the protestee read the *protest* or redress before beginning.
- no member of the protest committee is an *interested party*. Ask the *parties* whether they object to any member. When redress is requested under rule 62.1(a), a member of the race committee should not be a member of the protest committee.
- only one person from each boat (or *party*) is present unless an interpreter is needed.
- all boats and people involved are present. If they are not, however, the committee may proceed under rule 63.3(b).
- boat representatives were on board when required (rule 63.3(a)). When the *parties* were in different races, both

organizing authorities must accept the composition of the protest committee (rule 63.7). In a measurement *protest* obtain the current class rules and identify the authority responsible for interpreting them (rule 64.3(b)).

## L3    THE HEARING

**L3.1**    Check the validity of the *protest* or request for redress.

- Were the contents adequate (rule 61.2 or 62.1)?
- Was it delivered in time? If not, is there good reason to extend the time limit (rule 61.3 or 62.2)?
- When required, was the protestor involved in or a witness to the incident (rule 60.1(a))?
- When necessary, was 'Protest' hailed and a red flag flown correctly (rule 61.1(a))?
- When the flag and hail were not necessary was the protestee informed?
- Decide whether the *protest* or request for redress is valid (rule 63.5).
- Once the validity of the *protest* or request has been determined, do not let the subject be introduced again unless truly new evidence is available.

**L3.2**    Take the evidence (rule 63.6).

- Ask the protestor and then the protestee to tell their stories. Then allow them to question one another. In a redress matter, ask the *party* to state the request.
- Invite questions from protest committee members.
- Make sure you know what facts each *party* is alleging before calling any witnesses. Their stories may be different.
- Allow anyone, including a boat's crew, to give evidence. It is the *party* who must decide which witnesses to call. The question 'Would you like to hear N?' is best answered by 'It is your choice.'
- Call each *party's* witnesses (and the protest committee's if any) one by one. Limit *parties* to questioning the witness(es) (they may wander into general statements).
- Invite the protestee to question the protestor's witness first (and vice versa). This prevents the protestor from leading his witness from the beginning.
- Allow a member of the protest committee who saw the incident to give evidence (rule 63.6) but only in the presence of the *parties*. The member may be questioned and may remain in the room (rule 63.3(a)).

- Try to prevent leading questions or hearsay evidence, but if that is impossible discount the evidence so obtained.
- Accept written evidence from a witness who is not available to be questioned only if all *parties* agree.
- Ask one member of the committee to note down evidence, particularly times, distances, speeds, etc.
- Invite first the protestor and then the protestee to make a final statement of her case, particularly o n any application or interpretation of the *rules*.

L3.3 Find the facts (rule 63.6).

- Write down the facts; resolve doubts one way or the other.
- Call back *parties* for more questions if necessary.
- When appropriate, draw a diagram of the incident using the facts you have found.

L3.4 Decide the *protest* or request for redress (rule 64).

- Base the decision on the facts found (if you cannot, find some more facts).
- In redress cases, make sure that no further evidence is needed from boats that will be affected by the decision.

L3.5 Inform the *parties* (rule 65).

- Recall the *parties* and read them the facts found and decision. When time presses it is permissible to read the decision and give the details later.
- Give any *party* a copy of the decision on request. File the *protest* or request for redress with the committee records.

L4 **REOPENING A HEARING (Rule 66)**
When a timely request is made for a hearing to be reopened, hear the *party* making the request, look at any video, etc, and decide whether there is any material new evidence which might lead you to change your decision. Decide whether your interpretation of the *rules* may have been wrong; be open-minded as to whether you have made a mistake. If none of these applies refuse to reopen; otherwise schedule a hearing.

L5 **GROSS MISCONDUCT (Rule 69)**

L5.1 An action under this rule is not a *protest*, but the protest committee gives its allegations in writing to the competitor before the hearing. The hearing is conducted under the same rules as other hearings but the protest committee must have at least three members (rule 69.1(b)). Use the greatest care to protect the competitor's rights.

**L5.2** A competitor or a boat cannot protest under rule 69, but the protest form of a competitor who tries to do so may be accepted as a report to the protest committee which can then decide whether or not to call a hearing.

**L5.3** When it is desirable to call a hearing under rule 69 as a result of a Part 2 incident, it is important to hear any boat-vs.-boat *protest* in the normal way, deciding which boat, if any, broke which *rule*, before proceeding against the competitor under this rule.

**L5.4** Although action under rule 69 is taken against a competitor, not a boat, a boat may also be penalized.

**L5.5** The protest committee may warn the competitor when it believes this to be sufficient penalty, in which case no report need be made to the national authority. When the penalty is more severe and a report is made to the national authority, it is helpful to recommend to the national authority whether or not further action should be taken.

**L6** **APPEALS (Rule 70 and Appendix F)**
When decisions can be appealed,

* leave the papers so that the information can easily be used for an appeal. Is there an adequate diagram? Are the facts found sufficient? (Example: was there an *overlap*? Yes or No. 'Perhaps' is not a fact found.) Are the names of the protest committee members on the form, etc?
* comments on any appeal should enable the appeals committee to picture the whole incident clearly; the appeals committee knows nothing about the situation.

**L7** **PHOTOGRAPHIC EVIDENCE**
Photographs and videotapes can sometimes provide useful evidence but protest committees should recognize their limitations and note the following points:

* The *party* producing the photographic evidence is responsible for arranging the viewing.
* View the tape several times to extract all the information from it.
* The depth perception of any single-lens camera is very

poor; with a telephoto lens it is non-existent. When the camera views two overlapped boats at right angles to their course, it is impossible to assess the distance between them. When the camera views them head on, it is impossible to see whether an *overlap* exists unless it is substantial.

- Ask the following questions:

  - Where was the camera in relation to the boats?
  - Was the camera's platform moving? If so in what direction and how fast?
  - Is the angle changing as the boats approach the critical point? Fast panning causes radical change.
  - Did the camera have an unrestricted view throughout?

# APPENDIX M – INTERNATIONAL JURIES

*See rules 70.4 and 89(c). This appendix shall not be changed by sailing instructions or prescriptions of national authorities.*

## M1 COMPOSITION, APPOINTMENT AND ORGANIZATION

**M1.1** An international jury shall be composed of experienced sailors with excellent knowledge of the racing rules and extensive protest committee experience. It shall be independent of and have no members from the race committee, and be appointed by the organizing authority, subject to approval by the national authority if required (see rule 89(c)), or by the ISAF under rule 87.2.

**M1.2** The jury shall consist of a chairman, a vice chairman if desired, and other members for a total of at least five. A majority shall be International Judges. The jury may appoint a secretary, who shall not be a member of the jury.

**M1.3** No more than two members (three, in Groups M, N and Q) shall be from the same national authority.

**M1.4** (a) A jury of ten or more members may divide itself into two or more panels of at least five members each, of which the majority shall be International Judges. If this is done, the

requirements for membership of a full jury shall apply to
each panel but not to the jury as a whole.

(b) A jury of fewer than ten members may divide itself into two or more panels of at least three members each, of which the majority shall be International Judges. Members of each panel shall be from at least three different national authorities except in Groups M, N and Q, where they shall be from at least two different national authorities. If dissatisfied with a panel's decision, a party is entitled to a hearing by a jury composed in compliance with rules M1.1, M1.2 and M1.3, except concerning the facts found, if requested within the time limit specified in the sailing instructions.

**M1.5** When a full jury has fewer than five members, because of illness or emergency, and no qualified replacements are available, it remains properly constituted if it consists of at least three members. When there are three or four members they shall be from at least three different national authorities except in Groups M, N and Q, where they shall be from at least two different national authorities.

**M1.6** When the national authority's approval is required for the appointment of an international jury (see rule 89(c)), notice of its approval shall be included in the sailing instructions or be posted on the official notice board.

**M1.7** If the jury acts while not properly constituted, the jury's decisions may be appealed.

## M2 RESPONSIBILITIES

**M2.1** An international jury is responsible for hearing and deciding all *protests*, requests for redress and other matters arising under the rules of Part 5. When asked by the organizing authority or the race committee, it shall advise and assist them on any matter directly affecting the fairness of the competition.

**M2.2** Unless the organizing authority directs otherwise, the jury shall

(a) decide questions of eligibility, measurement or boat certificates; and

(b) authorize the substitution of competitors, boats, sails or equipment.

**M2.3**    If so directed by the organizing authority, the jury shall

(a)    make or approve changes to the sailing instructions,

(b)    supervise or direct the race committee in the conduct of the races, and

(c)    decide on other matters referred to it by the organizing authority.

**M3**    **PROCEDURES**

**M3.1**    Decisions of the jury shall be made by a simple majority vote of all members. When there is an equal division of votes cast, the chairman of the meeting may cast an additional vote.

**M3.2**    When it is considered desirable that some members not participate in discussing and deciding a *protest* or request for redress, the jury remains properly constituted if at least three members remain.

**M3.3**    Members shall not be regarded as *interested parties* (see rule 63.4) by reason of their nationality.

**M3.4**    If a panel fails to agree on a decision it may adjourn and refer the matter to the full jury.

# APPENDIX N – IMMEDIATE PENALTIES FOR BREAKING RULE 42

*This appendix applies only if the sailing instructions so state.*

**N1**    **PROTESTS**
A member of the protest committee or its designated observer who sees a boat breaking rule 42 may protest her by, as soon as reasonably possible, making a sound signal, pointing a yellow flag at her and hailing her sail number, even if she is no longer *racing*. A boat so protested is not subject to another *protest* under rule 42 for the same incident.

N2 **PENALTIES**

N2.1 **First Protest**
When a boat is first protested under rule N1 she may acknowledge her breach by taking a 720° Turns Penalty under rule 44.2. If she fails to do so she shall be disqualified without a hearing.

N2.2 **Second Protest**
When a boat is protested a second time during the series she may acknowledge her breach by immediately retiring from the race. If she fails to do so she shall be disqualified without a hearing and her score shall not be excluded.

N2.3 **Third Protest**
When a boat is protested a third time during the series she may acknowledge her breach by immediately retiring from the race and from all other races in the series. If she fails to do so she shall be disqualified without a hearing from all races in the series, with no score excluded, and the protest committee shall consider calling a hearing under rule 69.1(a).

N3 **POSTPONEMENT, GENERAL RECALL OR ABANDONMENT**
If a boat has been protested under rule N1 and the race committee signals a *postponement*, general recall or *abandonment*, the penalty from her first or second *protest* is cancelled, but the *protest* is counted to determine the number of times she has been protested during the series.

# APPENDICES, SECTION II

*The appendices of this Section, which are both ISAF regulations and racing rules, may be amended or changed at any meeting of the ISAF Council. Any amendment or change will be posted on the ISAF website (www.sailing.org) as soon as practicable and may be obtained directly from the ISAF.*

# APPENDIX 1 – ISAF ADVERTISING CODE

*See rule 79. This appendix shall not be changed by sailing instructions or prescriptions of national authorities. When governmental requirements conflict with parts of it, those requirements apply to the extent that they are more restrictive.*

## REGULATION 20

**20      ADVERTISING CODE**

**20.1    Definition of Advertising**
For the purposes of this code, advertising is the name, logo, slogan, description, depiction, a variation or distortion thereof, or any other form of communication that promotes an organization, person, product, service, brand or idea so as to call attention to it or to persuade persons or organizations to buy, approve or otherwise support it.

**20.2    GENERAL**

**20.2.1** Advertising shall not be displayed on a boat, except as required or permitted by the ISAF Advertising Code.

**20.2.2** Advertisements and anything advertised shall meet generally accepted moral and ethical standards.

**20.2.3** Advertisements on sails shall be clearly separated from national letters and sail numbers.

**20.3    ADVERTISING**

**20.3.1** The following types of advertising are permitted or required as stated and apply at all times:

# Appendix 1

(a) *Boats and Sailboards*

The class insignia shall be displayed on her sails as required by RRS Appendix G.

(b) (i) *Boats*

One sailmaker's mark, which may include the name or mark of the sailcloth manufacturer and the pattern or model of the sail, may be displayed on both sides of any sail and shall fit within a 150mm x 150mm square. On sails, other than spinnakers, no part of such mark shall be placed farther from the tack point than the greater of 300mm or 15% of the length of the foot.

(ii) *Sailboards*

One sailmaker's mark, which may include the name or mark of the sailcloth manufacturer and the pattern or model of the sail, may be displayed on both sides of the sail and shall fit within a 150mm x 150mm square. No part of such mark shall be placed farther from the tack point than 20% of the length of the foot of the sail, including the mast sleeve. The mark may also be displayed on the lower half of the part of the sail above the wishbone (boom) but no part of it shall be farther than 500mm from the clew point.

(c) (i) *Boats*

One builder's mark, which may include the name or mark of the designer, may be placed on the hull, and one maker's mark may be displayed on each side on spars and on each side of other equipment. Such marks shall fit within a 150mm x 150mm square.

(ii) *Sailboards*

Any number of manufacturers' names or logos may be placed on the board (hull) and in two places on the upper third of the part of the sail above the wishbone (boom). One maker's mark may be displayed each side on spars, and on each side of any other equipment.

(d) (i) *Boats*

The forward part of the hull on each side of all participating boats in an event shall only display advertising chosen and required to be displayed by that event organizer as follows:

– for boats under 6.5 metres, 25% of the *hull length*, and

– for boats over 6.5 metres, 20% of the *hull length*

excluding *bow numbers*. If such advertising is required, it shall be so stated in the Notice of Race. If advertising is for alcohol or tobacco, the word 'may' instead of 'shall' applies.

(ii) *Sailboards*
There shall be no reserved hull space on sailboards for event organizers.

The *organizing authority* of a sponsored event may permit or require the display of an advertisement of the event on both sides of the sail between the sail numbers and the wishbone (boom), on both sides of the sail aft of the foot median and on a bib worn by the competitors.

(e) competitors may display advertising on clothing and personal equipment without restriction.

**20.3.2** In addition to 20.3.1, additional advertising chosen by the individual boat may be displayed in the following categories:

(a) *Category A*
No additional advertising.

(b) *Category C*
Advertising is permitted as per Category A, and in addition on hulls, spars and sails without restriction except the space reserved for identification by Appendix G and under section 20.3.1(b), (c) and (d).

**20.3.3** When equipment is supplied by the event's *organizing authority*, Category C advertising on the supplied equipment is available to the *organizing authority*.

**20.4** All Classes (except when participating in events listed in Regulation 20.6) – ISAF and Non-ISAF Status, National Classes.

**20.4.1** The right to choose Category A or C applies to all ISAF *Classes*, except Olympic Classes which shall be unrestricted Category C.

**20.4.2** (a) The Class Associations of ISAF *Classes* may decide the advertising category to be applied to their class to be either A or C. If the Class Association makes no ruling, Category A shall apply.

(b) The Class Associations of Non-ISAF *Classes* (excluding *National Classes* referred to in Regulation 20.4.2(c) below) may decide the advertising category to be applied to their

Class to be either A or C. If the Class Association makes no ruling, Category A shall apply.

(c) For *National Classes* the National Authority of the *Class* decides Category A or C. If the National Authority makes no ruling, Category A shall apply.

**20.4.3** If Category C status is chosen, only the National Authority may introduce an Individual Advertising License System to permit its *competitors* to display advertising on their boats/sailboards. (A breach of a National Authority's license system is not protestable under this Code.)

**20.4.4** For *club* or *invitational events* the *organizing authority* may restrict advertising to Category A, with the approval of the National Authority of the organizing club.

**20.4.5** If Category C is decided, the ISAF Classes (except for Olympic Classes) and non-ISAF Classes (including *National Classes*) may decide the maximum level of advertising. Any restrictions within Category C shall be included in the Class Rules and subject to ISAF Council's approval. Olympic Classes cannot restrict Category C in anyway.

**20.4.6** Except as provided by Regulations 20.3.1 and 20.3.3 the right to have any or all advertising on the hulls, sails and spars shall be solely the right of and at the direction of the *competitor* provided that such right may be contracted or assigned to others at the competitor's discretion.

## 20.5 HANDICAPPING SYSTEMS AND RATING RULES

**20.5.1** The National Authority of a *competitor* in respect of the boat in which the *competitor* is competing, may decide the advertising category to be applied to boats racing under a handicap/measurement system to be either A or C. If Category C is decided, the said *competitor's* National Authority may decide the maximum level of advertising. If the National Authority makes no ruling, Category A shall apply.

Any 'Class' (see definition of Class) or individual boat racing under a handicap/measurement system shall have its advertising category determined in accordance with the provisions of this clause.

**20.5.2** For the purposes of Regulation 20.5.1, the provisions of Regulations 20.4.3, 20.4.4 and 20.4.6 shall apply.

**20.6    SPECIAL EVENTS/EVENTS OF CLASSES/ISAF EVENTS**

**20.6.1**  Category C applies.

**20.6.2**  ISAF will administer an Event Advertising System and/or Individual Advertising System for boats participating in the following events:

(i)    *Special Events*
America's Cup Match and Challenger/Defender Series
Volvo Ocean Race
Global Ocean Races
Trans-Oceanic Races
ORC World Championships
Professional Windsurfers Association Events (PWA)

(ii)   *Events of Classes*
International America's Cup Class
Volvo 60'
Maxi One Design
Open 60 Monohull Class (incorporates Open 50 Class)
Open 60 Multihull Class
PWA Classes
49'er Grand Prix series

(iii)  Proposals for other Special Events and/or Events of Classes of equal or similar status may, on the initiative of the Executive Committee or on application by an event *organizing authority* (with the approval of the relevant National Authority) to the Executive Committee and with its consent, be made to the Council for its approval.

(iv)   *ISAF Events*
ISAF World Youth Sailing Championship
ISAF Combined Olympic Classes World Championship
ISAF World Sailing Championship
ISAF Match Racing World Championship
ISAF Women's World Match Racing Championship
ISAF Team Racing World Championship
ISAF Women's Keelboat World Championship

And any other ISAF Events which may be introduced.

**20.7    FEES**

**20.7.1**  All boats carrying Category C advertising in line with Regulations 20.4 and 20.5 may be required to pay a fee only to their National Authority (no share to ISAF or any other National Authorities).

# Appendix 1

**20.7.2** All Events under Regulation 20.6 carrying Category C advertising shall pay a fee to ISAF (no share to any National Authority).

*Note: Sections 20.7.1 and 20.7.2 to be reviewed after 2 years (November 2003), before a final decision on the distribution of fees is decided.*

**20.8  ENTRY FEES**
There should be no variation of entry fees based on the *competitor's* category of advertising for the boat in which he is competing.

**20.9  Protests under this Code**

**20.9.1** When, after finding the facts, a protest committee decides that a boat or her crew has broken a section of this Code, it shall:

(a) give a warning; or
(b) disqualify the boat in accordance with RRS 64.1; or
(c) disqualify the boat from more than one race or from the series when it decides that the breach warrants a stronger penalty; or
(d) act under RRS 69.1 when it decides that there may have been a gross breach.

**20.10  DEFINITIONS**
The following definitions shall apply to this Code only:

Note: There are some definitions which are not needed in the present text of the Code.

(a) *'All Classes'*
Shall include all Classes as defined below and shall include Classes which are designated as ISAF Classes as well as Classes which are not designated as ISAF Classes.

(b) *'Class'*
A Class of boat/sailboard includes boats/sailboards which conform to a physical specification intended to allow competitive racing among the Class, and without limiting the generality of the foregoing, includes Classes with one-design, restricted, and developmental specifications as these terms are applied generally and for which there is an existing organization to administer the Class which has:

(i) an Executive or similar body which administers the Class,
(ii) a membership which is open to all owners of boats/sailboards which meet the specification of the Class, and

115

   (iii)   which holds a meeting of members at least once a year, and which gives notice of such meetings to all members.

(c)   *'National Class'*
A National Class for the purposes of this Regulation is a class where the National Authority has substantial authority in the direction or management of the Class.

(d)   *'Club or Invitational Event'*
A Club event is an event that is sponsored, organized or held by a Club which has sailing as one of its activities. An Invitational event is one in which the participants are invited and is not open to members of a participating class except by invitation.

A yacht club hosting an event which is a qualifier in any way for an International Class event cannot declare an Event Category 'A' by making the event an "invitational".

(e)   *'Hull Length'*
For the purposes of this Regulation, Hull Length is as defined in the applicable Class rules for Hull Length or any comparable measurement less Hull Appendages and if no means of measurement exists in the Class rules, Hull Length and Hull Appendage shall have the meaning set out in the Equipment Rules of Sailing, D.3.1 and E.1.1.

(f)   *'Organizing Authority'*
Shall have the definition contained in RRS 87.1.

(g)   *'Competitor'*
In addition to its natural meaning, a competitor in respect of any boat shall include any person who has the right to use the boat as owner or by charter, loan or otherwise.

(h)   *'Competitor Advertising'*
In respect of any boat is advertising which is applied to a boat, its equipment or the person or the equipment of a competitor or competitors as the condition of or as the result of a payment made to or made as a result of the direction of one or more of the competitors in respect of such boat.

(i)   *'Other Advertising'*
Advertising which is not competitor advertising.

(j)   *'Bow Number'*
An identifier assigned to a boat, usually for the duration of an event, by the organizer which is required to be dis-

played on the bow of a boat which may be a combination of numbers and letters.

*Note: Regulation 20 is subject to change by the ISAF Council. The current text of the regulation is available from the ISAF by mail, fax or e-mail (sail@isaf.co.uk).*

# APPENDIX 2 – ISAF ELIGIBILITY CODE

*See rule 75.2. This appendix shall not be changed by sailing instructions or prescriptions of national authorities.*

### REGULATION 21

### ISAF ELIGIBILITY CODE

**21.1    ISAF Eligibility Rules**
To be eligible to compete in an event listed in rule 21.2.1, a competitor shall:

(a)    be governed by the regulations and rules of the ISAF;

(b)    be a member of a Member National Authority or one of its affiliated organizations. Such membership shall be established by the competitor

   (i)    being entered by the national authority of the country of which the competitor is a national or ordinarily a resident; or

   (ii)    presenting a valid membership card or certificate, or other satisfactory evidence of identity and membership;

(c)    not be under suspension of ISAF eligibility.

**21.2    Events Requiring ISAF Eligibility**

**21.2.1**    ISAF eligibility is required for the following events:

(a)    the sailing regatta of the Olympic Games;

(b)    the sailing regattas of regional games recognized by the International Olympic Committee;

(c)    events including 'ISAF' in their titles;

(d)    world and continental championships of ISAF international classes and of the Offshore Racing Council;

(e)    any other event approved by the ISAF as a world championship and so stated in the notice of race and the sailing instructions;

(f) any event approved by a national authority or the ISAF as an Olympic qualifying event;

(g) all other international events involving an ISAF International Judge, Umpire, Race Officer or Measurer. For the purposes of this rule, international events are ISAF events, world and continental championships, and events described as international events in their notices of race and sailing instructions; and

(h) all events using the Racing Rules of Sailing.

**21.2.2** ISAF eligibility may be required for any other event when so stated in the notice of race and the sailing instructions with specific reference to this regulation.

**21.3    Suspension of ISAF Eligibility**

**21.3.1** After proper inquiry by either the national authority of the competitor or the ISAF Executive Committee, a competitor's ISAF eligibility shall be promptly suspended with immediate effect, permanently or for a specified period of time

(a) for any suspension of eligibility in accordance with RRS 69.2; or

(b) for breaking RRS 5; or

(c) for competing, within the two years preceding the inquiry, in an event that the competitor knew or should have known was a prohibited event.

**21.3.2** A prohibited event is an event:

(a) permitting or requiring advertising beyond that permitted by the ISAF Advertising Code;

(b) with prizes or other benefits referred to in Regulation 8.2 that is a national event not approved by the national authority of the venue or an international event not approved by the ISAF;

(c) that is described as a world championship or uses the word 'world', either in the title of the event or otherwise, and that is not approved by the ISAF; or

(d) that does not conform to the requirements of RRS 87, and is not otherwise approved by the ISAF.

**21.3.3** When an event described in rule 21.3.2 has been approved as required, that fact shall be stated in the notice of race and the sailing instructions.

**21.4    Reports; Reviews; Notification; Appeals**

**21.4.1** When a national authority suspends a competitor's ISAF eligibility under rule 21.3.1, it shall promptly report the suspension and reasons therefore to the ISAF. The ISAF Executive Committee may revise or annul the suspension with immediate effect. The ISAF shall promptly report any suspension of a competitor's eligibility, or of its revision or annulment by the ISAF Executive Committee, to all national authorities, international class associations, the Offshore Racing Council and other ISAF affiliated organizations, which may also suspend eligibility for events within their jurisdiction.

**21.4.2** A competitor whose suspension of ISAF eligibility has been either imposed by a national authority, or imposed or revised by the ISAF Executive Committee, shall be advised of the right to appeal to the ISAF Review Board and be provided with a copy of the Review Board Rules of Procedure.

**21.4.3** A national authority or the ISAF Executive Committee may ask for a review of its decision by the ISAF Review Board by complying with the Review Board Rules of Procedure.

**21.4.4** The Review Board Rules of Procedure shall govern all appeals and requests for review.

**21.4.5** Upon an appeal or request for review, the ISAF Review Board may confirm, revise or annul a suspension of eligibility, or require a hearing or rehearing by the suspending authority.

**21.4.6** Decisions of the Review Board are not subject to appeal.

**21.4.7** The ISAF shall promptly notify all national authorities, international class associations and the Offshore Racing Council of all Review Board decisions.

**21.5** **Reinstatement of ISAF Eligibility**
The ISAF Review Board may reinstate the ISAF eligibility of a competitor who:
(a) applies for reinstatement;
(b) establishes substantial, changed circumstances justifying reinstatement; and
(c) has completed a minimum of three years of suspension.

*Note: Regulation 21 is subject to change by the ISAF Council. The current text of the regulation is available from the ISAF by mail, fax or e-mail (sail@isaf.co.uk).*

# APPENDIX 3 – ISAF ANTI-DOPING CODE

See rule 5. This appendix shall not be changed by sailing instructions or prescriptions of national authorities.

### REGULATION 19

19 **ISAF ANTI-DOPING CODE**

The doping definition of the ISAF Medical Commission, like that of the International Olympic Committee (IOC), is based on the banning of pharmacological classes of agents.

The definition has the advantage that also new drugs, some of which may be especially designed for doping purposes, are prohibited.

The list published in Appendix 'A' of Olympic Movement Anti-Doping Code (OMADC) – and detailed at the end of Regulation 19 – represents examples of the different dope classes to illustrate the doping definition. Unless indicated, all substances belonging to the banned classes may not be used for medical treatment, even if they are not listed as examples. If substances of the banned classes are detected in the IOC accredited laboratory, the ISAF Medical Commission will report to the ISAF Executive Committee who will act upon the advice of the ISAF Anti-Doping Panel.

The presence of the drug in a sample of urine or blood constitutes an offence, irrespective of the route of administration.

Doping Controls shall be undertaken in the sport of sailing.

When governmental requirements conflict with parts of this ISAF Anti-Doping Code those requirements apply.

The following are basic ISAF requirements:

### PROCEDURES

**19.1 Selection of Competitors**

**19.1.1** A reasonable number of doping control tests, both in-competition (ICT) and out-of-competition (OOCT), shall be undertaken.

19.1.2 In-competition is defined as that period of time between the scheduled time of the warning signal of the first race of the event, up to the closure of protest time following the final race of the event.

19.1.3 Out-of-competition testing is defined as testing which takes place at other times outside the ICT period. When a doping control is conducted on the day of a competition in which the affected competitor has competed or is entered or expected to compete, the test shall be considered as in-competition. All other unannounced doping control shall be deemed to be OOCT. OOCT may be conducted by ISAF, by an ISAF authorized organization or on behalf and in collaboration with the World Anti-Doping Agency (WADA) or by WADA authorized organization at any time, or a recognized governmental agency, including at the time or location of any competition in every member country. Preferably it shall be carried out without any advance notice to the competitor or his/her Member National Authority (MNA).

19.1.4 ISAF and/or WADA may keep a register of competitors who are being subject to OOCT. Member National Authorities have the obligation to submit names, current places of living, addresses, telephone numbers, training times and training and competition locations for individuals and teams requested by ISAF and WADA, to enable ISAF and WADA to conduct OOCT.

19.1.5 ISAF and/or WADA can select competitors being subject to OOCT among all Member National Authority competitors. The selection can be done by ballot or any other principle that is decided by ISAF and/or WADA.

19.1.6 A competitor selected for sample taking shall not refuse to have a sample taken either in or out-of-competition, when required to do so by an accredited sampling officer acting on behalf of a Member National Authority, ISAF, WADA, IOC or a recognized governmental agency.

19.1.7 Doping Control is administered in order to uphold the requirements of RRS Fundamental Rule 5.

19.1.8 At an authorized event where doping control is undertaken, the protest committee chairman shall select competitors to be sampled on a specific day. Selection may be by means of a draw and specific competitors may be selected, as decided by the protest committee chairman. If on that day a race is postponed to a following day or abandoned, or if a competitor does not start in a race that is taking place, the protest committee chairman may still require the sampling of the specific competitor(s) already selected and may select any other competitors to be tested on that day. When there is more than one competitor in each boat, any or all of them may be selected. The race committee shall give to the sampling officer the names of the competitors selected for sampling. A competitor may be sampled more than once during an event.

### 19.2 Sample Taking

19.2.1 (a) The accredited sampling officer or his/her representative shall inform a competitor by written notice, which shall be given to the competitor, in confidence, that he or she has been selected for sample taking and is required to provide a urine or a blood sample at the time and place specified in the notice. The notice shall specify the name of the sampling officer appointed for the event (or OOCT) and of the designated laboratory (IOC accredited) to which the specimens will be sent.

(b) The competitor shall, during in-competition testing, sign an undertaking to be present at the Doping Control Station by a specific time, which will usually be not later than one hour after the time of notification. In back to back racing a competitor shall be notified at the conclusion of the race from which he/she has been selected, and extra time shall be allowed for the competitor to take part in any subsequent races that day, before returning to shore for Doping Control.

*After notifying the competitor the organizing committee representative for doping control should remain with the competitor at all times (unless racing) until they together arrive at the Doping Control Station.*

(c) The competitor may be accompanied by one person of his or her choice.

(d) A competitor who fails to appear at the appointed time and place, or who refuses to provide a sample shall be disqualified and sanctioned, together with the boat in which he or she was sailing, from the event and all the results to date shall be expunged. The protest committee shall call a hearing in accordance with RRS Part 5 Section B, to investigate the circumstances, to consider reasons offered to explain the failure to provide a sample in proper time, and report its findings to the initiating national authority, and to the national authority of the competitor.

19.2.2 The protocol for sample taking procedures at Doping Controls is detailed in Appendix 'C' of the OMADC.

19.2.3 The competitor and the accompanying person shall be attended in the waiting room of the Doping Control Centre by a member of the doping control team.

19.2.4 The member of the doping control team shall check the identity of the competitor and his/her sail number.

19.2.5 The time of arrival and personal data of the competitor shall be recorded.

19.2.6 Wherever possible only one competitor plus attendant/team official at a time should be called into the Doping Control Office. Where several tests are taking place this may not be possible.

19.2.7 In addition to the competitor and accompanying person only the following may be present in the Doping Control Office:

- A representative from ISAF;
- A member of the ISAF Medical Commission or their nominee;
- The officials in charge of taking samples and keeping records;
- An interpreter if required.

Photographs may not be taken in the Doping Control Station during the doping control procedure, unless required by the Doping Control Official in charge of the Doping Control Station. Representatives of the press are not allowed to be present during testing.

19.2.8 (a) When a competitor has been selected for OOCT the Sampling Officer (SO) appointed by ISAF or International Doping Control Officer (IDCO) appointed by WADA may either make an appointment to meet the competitor or, at preference, he/she may arrive unannounced to the competitor's training camp, accommodation or any other place where the competitor is likely to be found. In either case, the SO/IDCO shall provide proof of identity and provide a letter of appointment from ISAF or WADA. The SO/IDCO shall also require proof of identity of the competitor. The actual collection of the sample shall be in as much accordance with OMADC and Regulation 19 as is reasonable.

(b) Arrangements for collection of the sample shall be made as soon as possible after the appointment with the competitor has been made. It is the competitor's responsibility to check the arranged date, time and the precise location of the meeting.

(c) Where the SO/IDCO arrives unannounced he/she must give the competitor reasonable time to complete activity in which he/she is engaged, but testing should commence as soon as possible.

(d) In case a Team Doctor is not available or present at the OOCT, the competitor is responsible for declaring all medication taken by him/her in the 72 hours prior to the sample collection time. The Team Doctor does not need to be present to give written details or declare medication that the competitor is subject to. It is understood that the OOCT sample procedure is fully valid without the presence and without the declaration on the report form from the Team Doctor.

(e) Each competitor selected for OOCT shall, as part of the collection procedure, in conjunction with the SO/IDCO complete such laboratory forms as are required by the initiating authority or laboratory to whom the sample is to be dispatched.

(f) If the competitor refuses to provide a urine sample, the SO/IDCO shall note this on the doping control form used, enter his name on the form and ask the competitor to sign the form. The SO/IDCO shall also note any other irregularities in the doping control process.

(g) The nature of unannounced OOCT makes it desirable that little or no prior warning is given to the competitor. Every effort will be made by the SO/IDCO to collect the sample speedily and efficiently with the minimum of interruption to the competitor's training, social or work arrangements. If there is interruption, however, no competitor may take any action to gain compensation for any inconvenience incurred.

(h) If OOCT are conducted by WADA or by a WADA authorized organization, the original copy of the doping control form will be sent to ISAF and a copy will be kept in the possession of WADA.

(i) ISAF shall nominate a contact person responsible for the OOCT Testing liaison with WADA

(j) There has been signed an agreement between WADA and ISAF, the articles, terms and conditions of which are on record at ISAF. Under this agreement WADA will conduct OOCT services on behalf of ISAF in accordance with the OMADC and Regulation 19.

19.2.9  In ICT and OOCT the sampling procedure shall be carefully explained to the competitor in his/her own language or with the aid of an interpreter. It shall be made clear to the competitor that the sampling officer who directly supervises the passing of the urine sample shall be of the same sex as the competitor.

19.2.10  If the competitor refuses to provide a sample the possible consequences shall be explained to the competitor. If the competitor still refuses, this fact shall be noted in the records. These shall be signed by the official in charge of the station, the technician, representatives of the national authority which organized the sampling, and of any representative of ISAF who may be present and may be signed by the competitor and accompanying person. Following investigation the Member National Authority shall report findings and decisions relating to sanctions applied, to ISAF.

19.2.11  (a) The appropriately provided urine sample will be divided by the competitor into two samples 'A' and 'B' and placed in individual bottles which are sealed into individual containers. Codes shall identify the bottles and containers such that the laboratory does not know the name of any competitor.

(b) Samples collected during testing shall be forwarded in the appropriate sealed containers to the designated, IOC accredited, laboratory concerned. The sample taking, transportation and analysis shall be as detailed in Appendix 'C' of the OMADC. During transportation to the laboratory a record of the chain of custody shall be made from the time of production of the sample by the competitor to the time of opening of a container in the laboratory. At all times following its collection the sample shall be stored in the conditions required by the laboratory.

19.2.12  The analysis of sample 'A' shall be conducted by the accredited laboratory, and the result made available to the initiating authority, within 30 days of the taking of the sample at the Doping Control Centre.

19.2.13 The competitor shall provide a postal, fax or e-mail address at which during the 60 days following the taking of the sample required, he or she may be informed of the laboratory analysis results of sample 'A'. Should sample 'A' provide a positive result the address given will be used to inform the competitor, and to invite the competitor to attend or to be represented at the laboratory during the subsequent analysis of the 'B' sample. Sample 'B' shall be analysed within 10 days of the date of notification of the 'A' sample result.

Failure by a competitor to acknowledge receipt of the notice requiring his/her presence for the provision of a sample, or to sign the doping control form, or to provide a contact address will not be grounds for cancelling any penalty imposed for breaking RRS Fundamental Rule 5.

19.3 **Sample Analysis**

19.3.1 The Laboratory Analysis Procedures shall follow the protocol detailed in Appendix 'D' of the OMADC.

19.3.2 Analysis shall only be carried out in laboratories accredited by the IOC. Such laboratories are listed as Appendix 'C' to the OMADC and shall be regularly inspected to maintain accreditation standards.

19.3.3 Sample 'A' is analysed first. If sample 'A' is negative, ie. no proscribed medication or its metabolites are present, or no abnormal ratios or quantities for the presence of certain substances by the OMADC are noted, no further action is taken.

19.3.4 When 'A' sample is positive, ie. proscribed medication, metabolites or abnormal substance levels are noted:

(a) the initiating authority shall so inform the competitor and his/her national authority immediately. No race results shall be changed at this stage; and

(b) the laboratory will proceed to test sample 'B', the competitor or his/her representative may be present at the testing, and shall be informed of its time and place.

(c) when sample 'B' is negative, the initiating authority shall so inform the competitor and his/her national authority, no further action shall be taken.

(d) when no result has been obtained from sample 'B' after 60 days from the date of the sample taking, the procedure shall be considered void and no further action shall be taken.

(e) when sample 'B' is positive the initiating national authority, or ISAF in testing initiated by ISAF, will inform the competitor in writing at the address provided (see Regulation 19.2.13) and his/her national authority.

(f) any penalties imposed by the national authority against a competitor/participant who is found in breach of RRS Fundamental Rule 5, or of Regulation 19 shall be reported promptly to ISAF.

**19.3.5** Sanctions shall be applied in the first instance by the Member National Authority, which shall inform ISAF of its decisions. If the Member National Authority imposes no penalty, or an inadequate penalty, the possibility of imposing sanctions may be reviewed by ISAF.

**19.4 Penalties**

**19.4.1** The penalties for doping are stated in the OMADC.

**19.4.2** In addition to any penalty imposed under Regulation 21.3 a competitor who has found in breach of RRS Fundamental Rule 5 shall have his/her ISAF Eligibility suspended as provided in Regulation 21 – Eligibility Code.

**19.4.3** The competitor may appeal as provided in Regulation 21 and as Regulation 19.5.5 below.

**19.5 Hearings and Appeals Procedure**

**19.5.1** The competitor has 20 days from the date of the communication required by Regulation 19.3.4(e) to request a hearing or appeal to his/her Member National Authority, or to ISAF if the testing was initiated by ISAF.

**19.5.2** If no appeal has been lodged after the last day for any such appeal has passed, one or more of the penalties provided for in Regulation 19.4 will be applied with effect from the event during which the relevant testing took place and any subsequent event prior to the testing of the 'B' sample and during 20 days thereafter.

19.5.3 The findings of positive results shall be reported to ISAF, together with details of sanctions applied by the Member National Authority.

19.5.4 Competitors who have positive doping control results and who appeal against the finding of a breach of any of the anti-doping codes to which the competitor is subject or against the sanctions applied may be referred to the ISAF Anti-Doping Panel. The Anti-Doping Panel will consider evidence and report to the ISAF Executive Committee. The participant appealing is entitled to a copy of such procedures at the time he/she is notified of a positive result pursuant to Regulation 19.3.4(e).

19.5.5 Since ISAF recognizes the Court of Arbitration for Sport a participant may appeal the decision of the ISAF Executive Committee to the Court of Arbitration for Sport in accordance with the provisions for appeal of the Court. A copy of those provisions shall be provided to the participant at the time he/she is notified of the Panel's decision.

### 19.6 Exemptions

19.6.1 A competitor may request, only in writing, prior approval from the ISAF Medical Commission for the use of a banned substance, or a banned method, for special medical reasons. The reasons to be supported by written evidence from a specialist doctor. For the Olympic Games, dispensation can only be granted by the IOC Medical Commission, via an appeal made by the ISAF Medical Commission, the request to be made on behalf of the competitor, to ISAF, by his/her Member National Authority.

19.6.2 In Offshore races of more than 50 nautical miles, the use during a race of any banned substance or banned procedure for emergency medical treatment shall be reported promptly to the protest committee, which shall inform the appropriate national authority and the ISAF. The ISAF Medical Commission may retroactively approve such use.

### 19.7 Expenses

19.7.1 Any expenses in travel to observe analysis of a 'B' sample, or to give evidence on his/her own behalf, incurred in connection with this ISAF Anti-Doping Code by a competitor shall be his or her responsibility and neither the participant's National Authority or ISAF shall have any obligation for any such expenses.

19.8    **Team Doctors**

19.8.1  With the approval of ISAF or a Member National Authority or National Olympic Committee (NOC), a Team Doctor or a Doctor who is responsible for sailing competitors, officials and others in the care of that Doctor, may carry and employ such medications as the circumstances may require, and as might be expected to be properly used in the undertaking of the Hippocratic oath.

19.9    **Team Disqualification**

19.9.1  In the event that a competitor who is a member of a team is found guilty of doping, the boat upon which the offending sailor was a crew member shall be disqualified from the event. In sailing events in which more than one boat represents an individual national or other team, the boat upon which the offending sailor was a crew member shall be disqualified, but not other boats within a group of boats sailing as a team in either one or a number of classes.

19.10   **Declaration of Medications**

19.10.1 The use of the proscribed beta-2 agonists, which are classified as stimulants, is permitted, by inhalation only, in cases of proven asthma. They are permitted following written request, prior to an event, by the competitor to the relevant medical authority. The relevant doctor shall issue a certificate granting permission for the inhaler(s) to be used, and shall maintain a record of the issue of the certificate.

The relevant medical officer shall preferably be the Member National Authority doctor. In the event of the Member National Authority having no doctor appointed the request should be made to the ISAF Medical Commission.

Diabetics requiring insulin are also required to notify the relevant medical authority to obtain a certificate.

NOTIFICATION PROCEDURE

1.  *Competitors requiring treatment involving permitted beta-2 agonists by inhalation, or insulin, should note details of the treatment in writing, including diagnosis and the name and address of the prescribing physician.*

2.  *A copy of this information is sent in confidence to the Member National Authority Medical Officer, or in his absence to the ISAF Medical Commission.*

page

3. *The Member National Authority Medical Officer may wish to seek further information from the competitor or physician.*

4. *If diagnosis and treatment are accepted, the Member National Authority Medical Officer will send a certificate agreeing to the medication to the competitor, and maintain a record at the Member National Authority.*

5. *Further notification may be required, at intervals, for long term treatment.*

**19.11    Dispensation for taking Proscribed Medication**

19.11.1  If dispensation is requested for medication other than that listed in Regulation 19.10 above the Member National Authority Medical Officer will be required to request full medical details from the competitor, including diagnosis, names of specialists consulted, their address, hospital letters etc. These should be sent in confidence to the Chairman ISAF Medical Commission, with a request, backed by the Member National Authority, that dispensation for the taking of the listed medications be granted.

Following investigation such a dispensation may be granted by the ISAF Executive Committee for a fixed period subject to review. This will enable the sailor to compete in events held under ISAF rules.

19.11.2  For the Olympic Regatta dispensation can only be granted by the IOC, acting upon the advice of the IOC Medical Commission. To obtain this dispensation the Member National Authority should apply to the ISAF Medical Commission. The Member National Authority will be requested to provide full details as outlined above. The ISAF Medical Commission will then, if they agree to the request, submit a documented application to the IOC Medical Commission.

19.11.3  An ISAF Dispensation alone does not permit the sailor to compete in the Olympic Regatta.

**19.12    Classes of Prohibited Substances in Certain Circumstances**

19.12.1  Where in the OMADC in Appendix 'A' under III provides an option in the adoption of any substance on the proscribed list of medication, this choice of adoption will be made by the ISAF Executive Committee upon the advice of the Medical Commission.

**19.12.2** Pursuant to Regulation 19.12.1:

- Beta Blockers are permitted in sailing except for Match Race Helms

**19.13    ISAF Anti-Doping Panel**

**19.13.1** The ISAF Anti-Doping Panel will consist of:

- Executive Committee member – Chair
- Chairman, or alternative appointed by Chairman, of Medical Commission,
- Chairman, or alternative appointed by Chairman, of Racing Rules Committee,
- Chairman, or alternative appointed by Chairman, of Constitution Committee.

and may be called upon to consider breaches of the OMADC and Regulation 19 and then report to the ISAF Executive Committee.

---

*Note:  Regulation 19 is subject to change by the ISAF Council. The current text of the regulation is available from the ISAF by mail, fax or e-mail (sail@isaf.co.uk).*

The Olympic Movement Anti-Doping Code, Appendix A (IOC Prohibited Classes of Substances and Prohibited Methods), List of Examples of Prohibited Substances and Prohibited Methods, and other current information about the Code are also available on the ISAF website.

Received by race office: Number ............. Date and time ................................ Signed ....................................

----

**PROTEST FORM** – also for requests for redress and reopening

*Fill in and tick as appropriate*

**1.** EVENT ................................... Organizing authority............... Date ............... Race no ...

**2.** TYPE OF HEARING

Protest by boat against boat ❏   Request for redress by boat or race committee ❏

Protest by race committee against boat ❏   Consideration of reopening by protest committee ❏

Protest by protest committee against boat ❏   Consideration of redress by protest committee ❏

Request by boat or race committee to reopen hearing ❏

**3.** BOAT PROTESTING, OR REQUESTING REDRESS OR REOPENING

Class ...................................... Sail no...................... Boat's name ......................................................

Represented by ................................................ Address ...................................................... ...... Tel. .........

**4.** BOAT(S) PROTESTED OR BEING CONSIDERED FOR REDRESS

Class................................ Sail no. ................. Boat's name .............................................

**5.** INCIDENT

Time and place of incident ........................................................................................................

Rules alleged to have been broken ............... Witnesses ........................................................

**6.** INFORMING PROTESTEE   How did you inform the protestee of your intention to protest?

By hailing ❏ When? ........................ Word(s) used........................

By displaying a red flag ❏ When? .................................................................................

By informing her in some other way ❏ Give details ...........................................................................

**7.** DESCRIPTION OF INCIDENT (use another sheet if necessary)

DIAGRAM: one square = hull length; show positiion of boats, wind and current directions, marks

| THIS SIDE FOR PROTEST COMMITTEE USE | Number .............. Heard together with numbers ...

*Fill in and tick as appropriate*

Withdrawal requested ❑ ; signed ..................................................... Withdrawal permitted ❑

Protest time limit ...............................................................................

Protest, or request for redress or reopening, is within time limit ❑ Time limit extended ❑

Protestor, or party requesting redress or reopening, represented by ...............................................

Other party, or boat being considered for redress, represented by ...............................................

Names of witnesses ......................................................................................................

Interpreters ......................................................................................................

**Remarks**

Objection about interested party ❑ ...............................................

Written protest or request identifies incident ❑ ...............................................

'Protest' hailed at first reasonable opportunity ❑ ...............................................

No hail needed, protestee informed at first reasonable opportunity ❑ ...............................................

Red flag conspicuously displayed at first reasonable opportunity ❑ ...............................................

Red flag seen by race committee at finish ❑ ...............................................

Protest or request valid, hearing will continue ❑     Protest or request invalid, hearing is closed ❑

FACTS FOUND ...........................................................................................................................................

.................................................................................................................................................................

.................................................................................................................................................................

.................................................................................................................................................................

.................................................................................................................................................................

.................................................................................................................................................................

.................................................................................................................................................................

Diagram of boat ......................... is endorsed by committee ❑    Committee's diagram is attached ❑

## CONCLUSIONS AND RULES THAT APPLY

.................................................................................................................................................................

.................................................................................................................................................................

.................................................................................................................................................................

## DECISION

*Protest*  is dismissed ❑    Boat(s) ....................................................... is (are) disqualified ❑;

    penalized as follows ❑: ......................................................

*Redress* is not given ❑;    given as follows ❑: ........................................................................

Request to reopen a hearing  is denied ❑;    granted ❑

Protest committee chairman and other members ...............................................................................................

Chairman's signature ................................................................ ...........    Date and time .....................................

# EXPLANATORY SECTION

page

*(Red marginal page references)*

## Definitions

**Clear Astern and Clear
Ahead; Overlap**

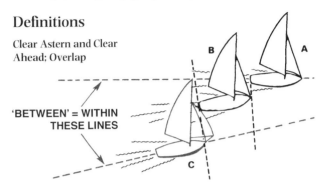

'BETWEEN' = WITHIN
THESE LINES

Watch out because a foresail, a spinnaker or a boomed-out jib could establish an overlap. The so-called 'transom line' is the critical overlap limit, but remember that it passes through the aftermost point of everything.

Boat B is 'between' A and C for the purpose of the definition, so C overlaps A if C overlaps B and B overlaps A. If boat B had been overlapping boat C and boat A, but on the far side of boat A, she would not have been a boat 'between' under this definition.

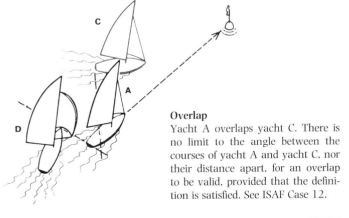

**Overlap**
Yacht A overlaps yacht C. There is no limit to the angle between the courses of yacht A and yacht C, nor their distance apart, for an overlap to be valid, provided that the definition is satisfied. See ISAF Case 12.

209

**Clear Astern and Clear Ahead; Overlap**

Red has not established an overlap because her spinnaker is not in the normal position.

**Not Overlap**

In this case, the definition says the boats are not overlapped. They are not on the same tack. Rule 10 applies.

**Overlap**

In this case, the boats are overlapped because Rule 18 applies.

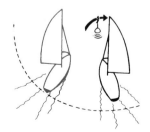

### Finishing and Racing
Even though the Red boat has received her winning gun, she would be disqualified for infringing Black because she has not cleared the finishing line and is still racing. See also the preamble of Part 2.

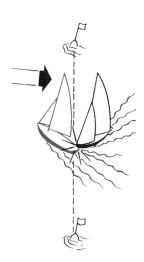

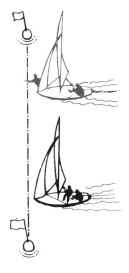

### Finishing
The rules say that the boat's crew has to be in normal position. The Red boat has not yet finished.

### Finishing
Red's spinnaker is not in its normal position and so she has not yet finished. See also Rule 31.2 for what happens when a boat touches a finishing mark. A further point to mention is that a race committee is not allowed to override the definition of finishing. See ISAF Cases 45 and 82.

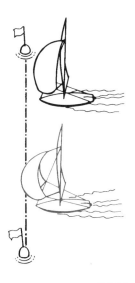

200

page

200

200

208

### Keep Clear

A keep-clear boat does not break a rule when touched by a right-of-way boat's equipment that unforseen suddenly moves out of normal position. See ISAF Case 77.

However, a keep-clear boat must keep clear of another boat's equipment that is out of normal position when possible because the equipment has been out of position long enough to be seen. See ISAF Case 91.

### Keep Clear; on the same tack

Red is overtaking. Black has right of way according to Rule 11. Normally Red would be keeping clear, if Black could sail her course, and Black could not change course without giving Red room to keep clear according to Rule 16. But as they are on the same tack the definition says that Red must keep a distance to Black that allows her not only to keep her course, but also allows room for Black to change course without immediately making contact. Thus Black has a possibility to luff to protect her wind and avoid being overtaken, but the right to luff is not as strong as in the old rules, even if Black has right of way. See also ISAF Case 60.

### Leeward and Windward Tack, Starboard or Port

Note that a boat is always on a tack, either starboard or port.

Tacking is not defined in the rules but is used in the common meaning of the word for the manoeuvre of changing tacks by passing head to wind. See also Rule 13.

Gybing means changing the mainsail from one side to the other with the wind from behind. When a boat tacks or gybes it changes momentarily from one tack to another.

### Leeward and Windward

Because these boats are not on the same tack, neither complies with the definition of windward boat or leeward boat.

page

### Leeward and Windward
Here neither boat is clear astern so the boats overlap. Black is on Red's leeward side so Black is the leeward boat and Red is the windward boat.

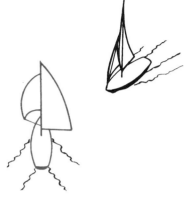

### Obstruction
A change of course is only substantial when a boat would lose a substantial amount of ground by altering course. A small fishing buoy, for example, would not cause any obstruction because it would just slide along the side of the boat without stopping it. But a small object such as a post or a buoy and objects such as heavy seaweed, floating plastic or timber could be an obstruction for the purpose of Rule 19 (Room to Tack). A racing boat is also an obstruction. See ISAF Case 41.

200

### Proper Course
The proper course is not necessarily the shortest course, there can be more than one 'proper course'. The criteria for a proper course is that the boat should have a valid reason for steering that course and applies it with some consistency. The end result has nothing to do with it. See ISAF Case 14.

Here, Black can bear away to sail the curved course to avoid the wind shade from the shore. See also ISAF Case 46.

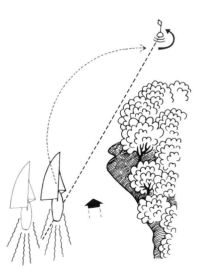

201

201

### Rules

All the different rules included in the definition *Rule* apply whether or not the NoR or SI so state. The only exceptions are the Prescriptions of a National Authority and Appendix A Scoring. These only apply when specifically stated in NoR or SI. See ISAF Case 98.

### Starting

This boat has crossed the line to start.

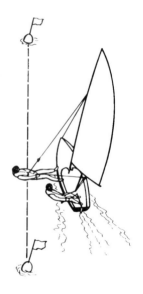

# SPORTSMANSHIP

Sportsmanship is not a rule that you can violate, it is part of the fundamental principles of the sport of sailing, however if you commit a gross
breach of a rule, of good manners, or of sportsmanship, the Protest
Committee may call a hearing under Rule 69, or Rule 2 (Fair Sailing).

The Racing Rules have no direct way of preventing a competitor who
has broken the Rules from continuing. But if you continue when you
are sure you have broken a rule, and for example interfere with
another competitor and force him to get a bad placing, you may be
commiting a gross breach of sportsmanship. See ISAF Case 65.

201

If you really have doubts as to who was right in an incident then you
should put up your protest flag. One or both boats could have been
wrong and it is best to resolve the issue so that you know what is
right next time. See ISAF Cases 1 and 68.

218

# PART 1 – FUNDAMENTAL RULES

**1.1 Helping Those In Danger**
It is very important that racing sailors help others in danger. Do not think somebody else will look after the distressed vessel or person – you must attend any incident unless you are completely sure your presence is no longer required. See ISAF Case 20.

You must, of course, also help your own crew when in danger, but this is not a reason for seeking redress under Rule 62.

**1.2 Life-Saving Equipment and Personal Buoyancy**
Note also that according to Rule 40 neither wet nor dry suits are acceptable as personal buoyancy.

**2 Fair Sailing**
Note that this rule also applies when *not* racing; a crew might deliberately damage a boat between races during a series. You can be disqualified between races, or you could be disqualified for a whole series. ISAF Cases 34, 47, 65, 73, 74 and 78 contain further interpretations of this rule.

**3 Acceptance of the Rules**
When participating in sailboat racing you accept that the decisions according to the ISAF Rules, including Appeals etc. described in the Rules, are final and cannot be referred to a court of law. See also the definition of Rules.

**4 Decision to Race**
The responsibility of whether or not a boat races must rest finally with the boat and her crew. The organisers cannot be blamed or held responsible for not abandoning a race because of bad weather.

**5 Drugs**
Be careful what drugs you take. Many non-prescription drugs are banned.

# PART 2 – WHEN BOATS MEET

This is the most tricky part of the Racing Rules, and so we will spend some time in examining cases in detail.

Remember that if you are racing and meet another boat racing, these Racing Rules apply. It does not matter if the boats are in different races. If you are not sure that the other boat is racing then the International Regulations for Preventing Collisions at Sea apply (otherwise known as 'Rules of the Road at Sea'), which all normal shipping has to recognise. These regulations always take precedence if there is any doubt. See ISAF Case 67.

203

Take note that the IRPCS could be enforced in a race held between sunset and sunrise if so stated in the Sailing Instructions. See ISAF Case 38.

203

In order to settle any damage claims, the result of a boat racing protest is normally binding on two boats racing. If one or both boats are not racing then liability depends on the 'Rules of the Road at Sea'. See also Rule 3.

Note that the penalty limitations in the preamble of Part 2 only apply to the rules of Part 2, except Rule 22.1. Before you go afloat you should study the Sailing Instructions very carefully because you can be disqualified if you fail, at any time, to keep any of the other rules for a particular race or event. For example, you may be required to carry some special flag in your rigging; you may be required to wear lifejackets; there may be some special instructions going to and from the race area; or you may have to carry extra buoyancy.

To help you identify the numbers of a particular rule in Part 2, refer to the Fast Find Diagram on page 2

page

## Section A – Right of way

10 **On Opposite Tacks**
Port and starboard incidents without contact are very common. There is no requirement in the Rules for the onus to be on the port tack boat to prove he was clear of the starboard tack boat but conversely there is nothing in the Rules to suggest that the starboard tack boat should hit the port tack boat to prove her point. See ISAF Case 50.

203

204
211

ISAF Cases 23, 30, 43 and 88 contain further interpretations of this rule.

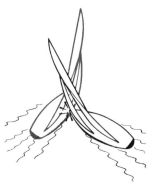

10 **On Opposite Tacks**
Black has the wind coming from the starboard side and Red has the wind from the port side. Thus Red should keep clear of Black.

10 &
16 **Changing Course**
Red must not luff to try to hit Black, who would otherwise have been able to keep clear. This case comes under Rule 16.1.

page

10    Even though Black is 'overtaking' Red (Fig 1), the definition of 'clear astern' is not valid because they are on opposite tacks and so Rule 10 applies. Red must give way because Black is on starboard tack.

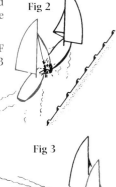

Fig 1

10 &    Here (Fig 2) they are subject to Rule
18.2(b)  18 and Red must keep clear even if she is on starboard tack because Black is within two of her overall lengths of an obstruction. See also ISAF Case 30.

211

11    **On the Same Tack, Overlapped**
Red is the windward boat (Fig 3) and therefore has to keep clear of Black. See also definition of Keep Clear.

Fig 2

Further examples are covered in ISAF Cases 7, 13, 14, 24, 25, 51, 70, 73 and 74

206
204
201
205
208
202

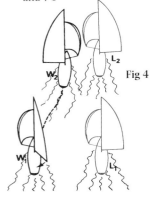

Fig 4

Fig 3

10 &    **Changing Course.** W and L are running parallel (Fig 4), over-
16.2    lapped, on port tack. W gybes on to starboard. Rule 15 applies only briefly after S becomes right-of-way boat, but even if the boats now sail parallel for some time and L is no longer protected by Rule 15, W must still be very careful when she changes her course. Not only must she give L room under Rule 16.1 but if a change of course from W makes it necessary for L to respond immediately to keep clear, W would break Rule 16.2. So Rule 16.2 gives more protection to the keep-clear boat and ISAF Case 18 that disqualified L in this situation is deleted.

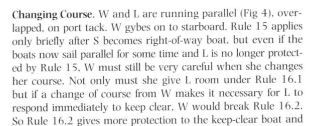

**11 &** **Same Tack, Definition Keeping Clear and**

**16** **Changing Course**

Black can luff slowly head to wind. She has to give Red room to keep clear when she luffs (Rule 16.1), but Red has to keep clear as windward boat (Rule 11) and this includes keeping clear so Black can change course (luff) without immediately making contact (def. Keep Clear). ISAF Case 52 is relevant in a match race situation.

207

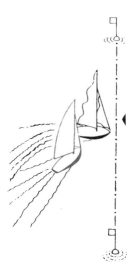

**11** **On the Same Tack, Overlapped**

Black may luff slowly head to wind, even if Red is forced over the line early. Black must give Red enough time and room to keep clear. After the signal Black's rights depend on how the overlap was established and her proper course. See Rule 17.1 and ISAF Case 13.

204

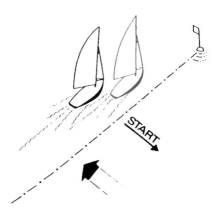

**11 & 17 Proper Course and Definitions**

Before the starting signal there is no proper course; after the signal. Rule 17.1 applies depending on how the overlap was established.    Black can luff slowly head to wind and Red has to keep clear.

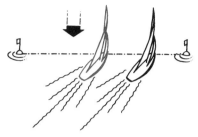

page

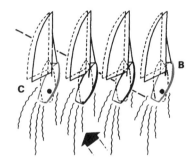

**11 & 16    Changing Course**

Even if C has the right of way under Rule 11 and is not prohibited by Rule 17.1 to sail above proper course, in practice her possibility to luff is very limited when there are more boats to windward. Under Rule 16.1 she must give the windward boats room to keep clear when she is changing course. If there are several boats to windward it might not be possible for C to luff at all because of the delay in response from the other boats. B and C are still overlapped because of the boats 'between'. See definition Clear astern, Overlap.

**12    On the Same Tack, Not Overlapped**

Red must keep clear and must not sail into Black's stern, if they are on the same tack.

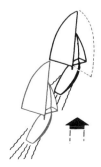

149

page

205

13    **While Tacking**
This boat has no right of way until
she reaches a close-hauled course.
She is on close-hauled even if the sail
is not full because the main-sheet is
too loose. Whether the boat has
movement through the water or not,
is irrelevant. See ISAF Case 17.

206

13    **While Tacking and**
15    **Acquiring Right of Way**
Red tacks on to starboard and must come on close-hauled
course before she can claim right-of-way over Black. Black does
not have to begin to give way until Red is on close- hauled
course and she is not required to anticipate that Red will break
a rule. See ISAF Case 27.

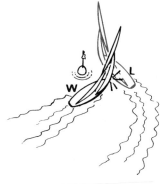

| 13 | Tacking |
| 14 | Avoiding Contact |
| 15 | Acquiring Right of Way and |
| 16 | Changing Course |

Here Black bore away to pass under Red's stern. When Red saw this she tacked. There was a collision and Red was wrong under Rule 13 (While Tacking).

Rule 10 ceased to apply when Red passed head to wind and thus stopped being the right-of-way boat.

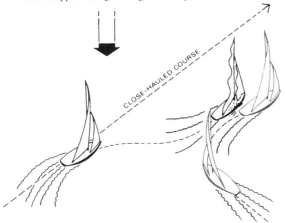

Red became right-of-way boat again when she came on close-hauled, but in such a case Black would not have to *begin* to take avoiding action until Red was on close-hauled (or when it is clear that Red is not keeping clear, Rule 14) and Red shall initially give Black room to keep clear (Rule 15). Had Red been able to tack coming on close hauled in an ample distance to the leeward of Black, Red would have been in the clear. See ISAF Case 6.

207

| 13 | **Two Boats Tacking** |

In this case the Red boat, which is on Black's port side, must give way. Remember it like this 'If you are on the right – you are in the right!'

page

## Section B – General Limitations

**14** **Avoiding Contact**
Any boat shall avoid contact, and can be penalised for not trying to avoid it, even if she has right-of-way. If the right-of-way
boat tries to avoid contact and fails, and the contact does not
result in damage 'that would ordinarily be promptly repaired',
then she is still in the clear. However, if the contact causes
damage, a right-of-way boat can still be penalised. See ISAF
Case 19.

206

There is no rule that demands hailing before an unforeseen
alteration of course, but hailing could still be one way of
'avoiding contact with another boat if reasonably possible',
so it is wise to hail.

201
204
205
211
203
214
207

ISAF Cases 14, 23, 26, 30, 50, 54, 87 and 92 contains further interpretations of this rule.

**15** **Acquiring Right of Way by
establishing an Overlap from
Clear Astern.**
Before the start the Red boat
came from astern with better
speed. Red obtained the overlap too close to Black who
was not given enough room
by Red to luff to keep clear.
Red is wrong under Rule 15.
See ISAF Case 53.

206

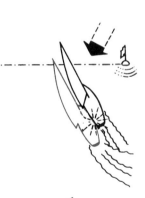

**15** **Acquiring Right of Way by
establishing an Overlap.**
In this case Red has also overtaken Black and has initially
given too little room for Black
to be able to luff and keep
clear, because Black's stern
will swing to port as she luffs.
See also ISAF Cases 7 and 24.

206

15 **Acquiring Right of Way**
11 **Overlapped and**
17.1 **Same Tack Proper Course**

The Black boat is overtaking. From the moment that Black gains an overlap the Red boat becomes the 'windward' boat. She must then start to luff far enough so that Black does not touch her boom, but she need not luff any further because Black must not sail above her proper course. See ISAF Cases 7 and 24.

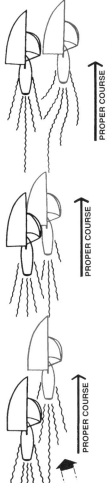

page

206

15 **Acquiring Right of Way by Gybing**

When Red gybes she gains right-of-way and can force Black to alter course. However here Red has gybed too late and must initially give Black room to keep clear.

▼

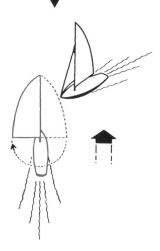

153

15
13
**Acquiring Right of Way by Tacking and While Tacking**

Red is coming on port tack and is tacking on to starboard tack. Until Red is on close-hauled she shall keep clear under Rule 13. After Red is on close-hauled she must initially give Black room to keep clear. Black does not have to start to luff until after this moment and is therefore right.

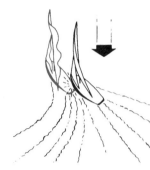

15
**Acquiring Right of Way**

This situation is also covered by Rule 15. A hail from Black when she is close-hauled will clarify the moment when she gains the right to force Red to start avoiding a contact. Red does not have to start any avoiding action until Black is on close-hauled, unless it is clear that there will be contact if she does not act before (Rule 14 Avoiding Contact).

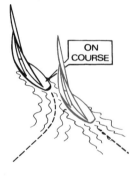

ON COURSE

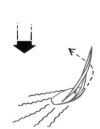

15
**Acquiring Right of Way**

In this situation the Red boat tacks but there is no possibility of D being able to clear Red after Red has completed her tack, and D can not tack herself because of the proximity of the other boats. Red has not satisfied Rule 15. If the Red boat was to tack on to starboard she would have to bear away astern of D.

**15 &**
**19.1**   Room to Tack

In this situation if the Black boat (on the right) tacks, the Red boat can only bear away (and give room to B and A under Rule 18.2 if they have an overlap). This is because there is no time for B and A to respond after a hail from Red before a collision would occur with Black.

**15**   Acquiring Right of Way
**13**   While Tacking and
**14**   Avoiding Contact

What does the Protest Committee do? Red protests. Black is the give-way boat before the tack (Rule 10) while tacking (Rule 13) and she has initially to give room to Red (Rule 15). There is no longer in the rules an onus for Black to prove that she was not too close. However the Protest Committee will often go with Red, first because Black created the situation and second, to stress the importance of the 'basic' rules. So it is easy for Red to put in a protest in a case like this, even if Black was not very close. Black should keep this in mind before making the manoeuvre (or have good witnesses). On the other hand, if Red can touch Black without bearing away, she ought to win the protest. Red does not have to begin to luff clear until Black is on a close-hauled course.

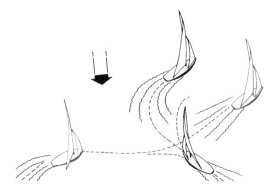

#### 16.1 & 16.2   Changing Course

Red has borne away to pass under Black's stern. In order to avoid breaking Rule 16.2, Black must neither luff to tack nor bear away in order to make it difficult for Red to keep clear ('hunting') if this means that Red would immediately need also to change course to keep clear. When the boats get even closer so that any change of course from Black would deny Red room to keep clear, Black would also break Rule 16.1. If Black does not start to luff for her tack until Red can pass behind her without changing course further, Black would not break Rule 16 but must keep clear while tacking. There may be some doubt as to the actual change of course from Black, but if it is clear that Black has changed her course the onus will be on Black to show that Red did not immediately have to alter course further to keep clear. Red only has to act on the course Black is steering at the time to keep clear. She is not supposed to expect Black to 'hunt' and subsequently change her course. See ISAF Case 92

207

#### 16.1 & 16.2   Changing Course and
#### 13   While Tacking

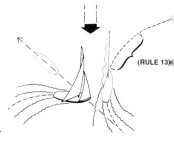

(RULE 13)

If the Red boat luffs head to wind and Black must immediately change course to keep clear, Red can be disqualified under Rule 16.2 and maybe also 16.1, depending on the distances between the boats. If she goes further and tacks, she can be disqualified under both Rules 16 and 13, depending on where the incident actually occurred. See also ISAF Case 6.

207

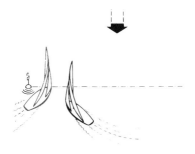

## 16 Changing course to start

Red is trying to make a port tack start. Even if Black is right-of-way she must remember that if she luffs at the signal to assume proper course she must give Red room to keep clear under Rule 16. If Red has timed her start perfectly and is on a steady course that would keep her clear of Black before Black luffs, she is OK, but it is a risky manoeuvre for Red. *Note!* there is no longer a rule that allows Black to assume proper course even if this prevents Red from keeping clear.

## 16 Changing Course Rounding a Mark

Red takes the mark rather wide and tacks. Black is clear astern but rounds tighter and can touch Red. Red must give way under Rules 13 and 10, but if Red could have kept clear of Black while tacking and after getting on port tack, had Black not changed her course round the mark, Red is protected by Rule 16. *Note!* there is no longer a rule that allows Black to assume proper course round-ing a mark even if this prevents Red from keeping clear.

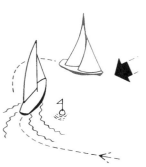

See ISAF Case 76 for a situation where the starboard boat is changing course at a windward finishing mark.

208

If a right-of-way boat alters course in such a way that the give-way boat, in spite of prompt avoiding action, still cannot keep clear by her own efforts then the right-of-way boat breaks Rule 16. See ISAF Case 60.

208

# Rule 17

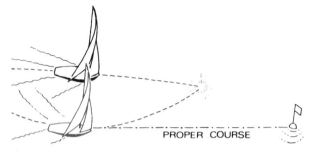

PROPER COURSE

### 17.1 On the Same Tack; Proper Course

Red establishes her overlap by diving through the Black boat's lee but must not sail above her proper course whilst the overlap lasts. If there is a dispute about what is the proper course then the Black boat must keep clear. See ISAF Cases 14 and 46, and also explanations of Proper Course.

### 17.1 On the Same Tack;
### Proper Course
**Definition: Clear Astern**

Black is overtaking Red and is the give-way boat because she is on port. As soon as her bow crosses Red's 'transom-line', she may gybe and then gains the right to sail above a proper course. If Black was overtaking on the same tack as Red, then she could gain the right by doing two quick gybes.

PROPER COURSE

**17.1** **On the Same Tack; Sail
Above Proper Course**
Black must gybe if the overlap was established from
clear astern, because gybing
is the only way she can
avoid sailing above her proper course. This is also in
accordance with Rule 18.4.
See also ISAF Case 75.

page

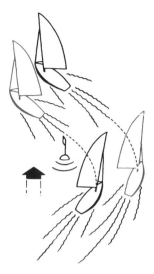

213

**17.2** **On the Same Tack; Sail
Below Proper Course**
Black is inside a distance of
two of Red's lengths from
Red. Red must not bear
away from her proper course
to interfere with Black if it is
a free leg of the course.

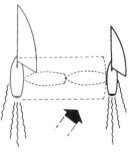

**17.1 &
17.2** The two-length limitation applies only to these rules. The
measurement of the two boats' length distance is taken from
hull to hull as shown.

## 17.1 & 11    Same Tack Overlapped

B is overtaking D with better speed on a steady course which is slightly higher than the course to the next mark. She is not 'changing course'. D should call 'Overlap!' and thus B cannot sail above her proper course as this overlap exists. B is *not* obliged to bear away to the mark. She is actually sailing *her* 'proper course', and Rule 11 applies. If D thinks that B is sailing above her proper course, her only remedy is to keep clear and protest. See also definition of Proper Course and ISAF Case 14.

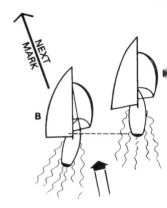

## 17.2 11    Sail Below Proper Course and Overlapped

If the leg is to windward, Rule 17.2 does not apply, Red may bear away towards Black's course but if she touches she will be disqualified under Rule 11. If a tack will have to be made to reach the next mark this is evidence that you are on ' a beat to windward'.

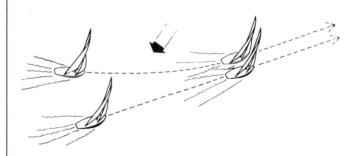

17.1,
11 &
12    **Stopping a luff**

It is clever to call 'No overlap!' or something similar, as soon as the overlap is broken, because this is the best way to stop the leeward boat sailing above her proper course. When Red becomes clear ahead the Black boat must keep clear under Rule 12 and Red can bear away to her proper course. When the overlap is re-established it will be from clear astern so even if Black is again right of way she cannot sail above her proper course. Black can only regain her right to sail above her proper course if she creates a new overlap by drawing clear ahead or more than two lengths abeam, or by doing two quick gybes.

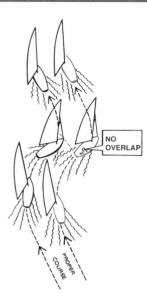

page

# Section C – At Marks and Obstructions

All Rules in this section cover special cases. When these cases apply they sometimes override or modify the basic rules which precede them in Section B of Part 2.

18    **Room to Pass Marks or Obstructions**

This is one of the most important rules, as it is the one that is involved most frequently. It is set out in three parts.

18.1    Instructions on where the Rule applies, and special situations where it does not (or where only part of it applies). At a starting mark and when beating on opposite tacks.

18.2,
18.3 &
18.4    The Rule itself, with instructions for giving room and keeping clear when rounding and passing, including what happens if one boat tacks or has to gybe.

18.5    Limitations on establishing an overlap in the case of a continuing obstruction.

## 18.1 About to Pass

As soon as you are 'about to pass ' the mark and an inside boat has an overlap, Rule 18 starts to apply and the outside boat must give room. 'About to pass' is usually interpreted as two lengths, but for fast planing dinghies or catamarans, it might be more. See ISAF Case 84. Also note that even if the boats have become 'about to pass' more than two lengths from the mark, the overlap relation can still change and it is only at the two-length zone that it is decided whether 18.2(b) or (c) will govern the rounding. See ISAF Case 94.

### Taking an Inside Boat the Wrong Side of a Mark

If you wish to take a windward boat to the wrong side of the mark you may do so, but you must (1) be (at least) more than two boat lengths from the mark and (2) have the right to sail above proper course (Rule 17.1).

### 18.1(a) Not at a Starting Mark

B has no right to room at a starting mark. Rule 11 covers the situation. Until the starting signal A can sail up head to wind and B must keep clear. As soon as the starting gun has fired, A must not sail above a proper course if her overlap was established from clear astern (Rule 17.1) and must not squeeze B out by sailing higher than this.

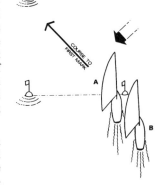

If there is still not enough room for B then A is not obliged to sail lower than proper course because Rule 18 does *not* apply at a starting mark, but 17.1 does.

### 18.1(a) Not at a Starting Mark

Black cannot claim room at a starting mark under Rule 18. However Black has the right under Rule 11 to luff and try to 'shoot the mark', as long as she gives Red room to keep clear, as provided by Rule 16, and does not pass head to wind.

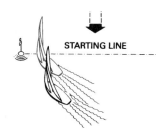

**18.1,**
**11 &**
**17.1**    Yacht C can neither claim room between boat D and
the mark under Rule 18 before the starting gun nor
afterwards. Rules 11 and 17.1 apply.
Yacht A is head to wind and
has the right to do this before
and after the starting gun if
the overlap was *not* established from clear astern. After
the signal he must not sail
above a proper course if she
established the overlap from
clear astern. Rules 11 and
17.1 cover the situation.

**18.1(b)  Not on Opposite Tacks**
This clause says that Rule 18
does not apply in this situation because the two boats
are sailing to windward on
opposite tacks. Rule 10
applies, and so Black does not
have to give room to Red to
round a mark inside her.

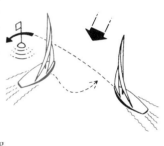

**18.1(b)  Opposite Tacks and**
**18.3      Tacking**
Red cannot claim room
under Rule 18.2 while luffing
or 'While Tacking' (Rule
13) though she may have
rights both before (Rule 10)
and after. If Red chooses to
sail past the mark Black
must keep clear under Rule
10. It is exactly the same as
if they were in the middle of
the course with no mark
anywhere near.

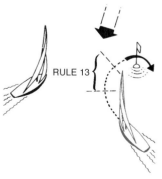

Remember it like this: at the
windward mark on opposite
tacks, take the mark away.
See also ISAF Case 9.

page

209

### 18.2(a) Overlapped – Basic Rule

Red shall give room to Black, assuming Black made her overlap in time. Red must give room even though both boats are on widely differing courses. See ISAF Case 12.

209

### 18.2(a) Overlapped – Basic Rule

Black must have enough room to be able to gybe without being obstructed by Red, because the gybe is part of passing the mark. Red must still keep clear even if Black's gybe breaks the overlap. See also ISAF Case 21 for interpretation of 'room'.

209

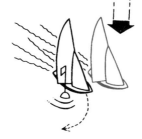

### 18.2(a) Overlapped – Basic Rule

Black must have room to be able to tack, if the tack is necessary to *pass* the mark. If Black's genoa touched Red when it was freed off for tacking, for example, Red would not have given enough room. If the mark is rounded as the start of a 'windward leg', Black is only entitled to room to pass the mark and initially to assume a 'close-hauled' course. She is then the windward boat (Rule 11) and cannot claim room for a tack that she wants to make for tactical reasons. See ISAF Case 25.

205

NEXT
MARK

**18.2(a)  Overlapped – Basic Rule and**
**19        Room to Tack**
          The starboard tack boat is an obstruction. Red can elect to tack
          or to bear away. If she elects to tack, Rule 19 applies. If she
          elects to bear away, Rule 18 applies, and she has to give room

page

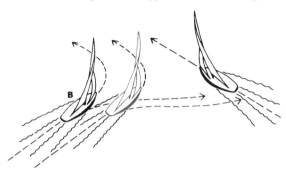

          to boat B who is overlapping 'inside'. It is Red who can choose
          what she wants to do, because she has right of way over B as
          the leeward boat under Rule 11. See also Rule 19 and ISAF
          Cases 3 and 11.

214
209

**18.2(a)  Overlapped – Basic Rule**
          The boat not racing is crossing the course, and Red must
          give Black room to pass on the same side as herself.

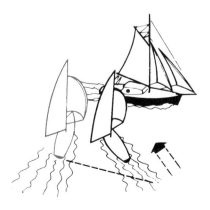

page

**18.2(a)  Overlapped – Basic Rule**
**18.2(b)  Overlapped at the zone**

When a boat comes abreast of a mark but is more than two lengths from it, and when her alteration of course towards the mark results in a boat previously clear astern becoming overlapped inside her when she enters the two-lengths zone. Rule 18.2(a) requires her to give room to that boat. Red shall continue to give Black room even if the overlap is broken and when she becomes clear astern she shall also keep clear and is not entitled to room even if she tries to sail inside Black.

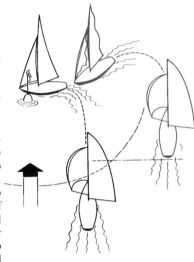

210
211

See also ISAF Cases 59 and 2.

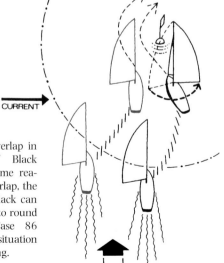

CURRENT

**18.2(b)  Overlapped at
the zone**

Black has an overlap in time. Even if Black gybes, or for some reason loses the overlap, the rule says that Black can still claim room to round inside. ISAF Case 86 covers a similar situation in a port rounding.

210

### 18.2(a) Overlapped

Red is not within the limit distance of two boat lengths of the mark when she alters course and thus 'gives' Black an overlap when Red enters the circle. She cannot refuse to give Black room, because the overlap is established in time. However, see also 18.2(e): If there is doubt about establishing an overlap in time.

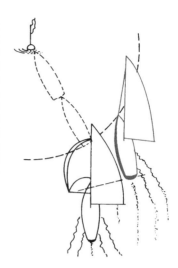

### 18.2(a)
### 11 &
### 17.1

If Black has established her overlap outside the zone, or because of Red tacking on top, Red must keep clear. Even if Rule 17.1 applies between them, Black can luff above close-hauled to 'shoot the mark'. This is her 'proper course' so Red is give-way boat, both according to Rule 18 and according to Rules 11 and 17.1. There is no conflict between the rules.

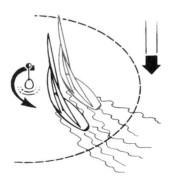

In the case of a starboard rounding, Red must still keep clear under Rule 11 and cannot force Black to bear away until they are so close to the mark that Red is being denied room by Black. See ISAF Case 70.

208

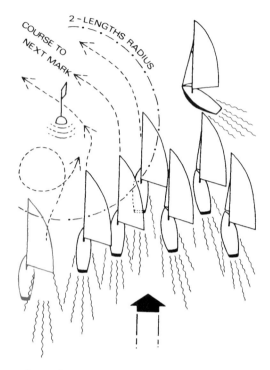

COURSE TO
NEXT MARK

2-LENGTHS RADIUS

### 18.2(e) Overlap Rights

Even though Red has established an overlap before the next boat entered the two-length zone, the latter may not be able to give room because of the delay in response from the outside boats. If Black is not able to give room at the time when the overlap begins, Rule 18.2(a) and (b) does not apply and Red is not entitled to room.

**18.2(c)** Not Overlapped at the zone

**18.2(d)** Changing Course to Round or Pass

Black is allowed to make a normal smooth rounding. She is within a radius of two boat lengths of the mark and is also clear ahead of Red and so she does not have to give room inside. Also Rule 16 does not apply when she is altering course to round the mark.

Black is protected under Rule 18.2(c) until both boats have completed the rounding manoeuvre. See ISAF Case 62.

If Black makes a bad rounding, maybe because of boats ahead of her, and gives Red room, Red may try to round inside, but at her own risk. See ISAF Case 63.

page

212

212

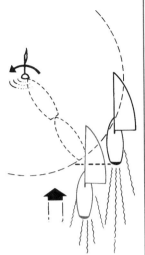

**18.2(c)** Not Overlapped

Red must keep clear even though she now has an overlap if this was not made in time. Neither can Red claim her starboard tack rights because Black is inside the two-boat-length circle and Rule 18 takes precedence over Rule 10.

**18.2(c)** Not Overlapped

Black, who is clear ahead, has the right to gybe. This is part of the passing manoeuvre and so Red must keep clear until Black has gybed and passed the mark.

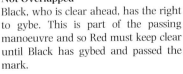

page

211

212

211

**18.2(c)** Not Overlapped and
**13** While Tacking

Red is clear ahead but cannot claim room to tack because 18.2(c) says that if she passes head to wind Rule 18.2(c) no longer applies and Rule 13 is the correct rule. See ISAF Case 15.

The rights are the same if the situation is reversed to a starboard rounding. See ISAF Case 81.

**18.2(c)**
**13** While Tacking and
**16** Changing Course

If Black thinks she is far enough ahead to be able to tack and clear Red without causing her to alter course, she can do so. Black has right of way while she luffs. When she passes head to wind she becomes give-way under Rule 13, but Red must then under Rule 16 not change her course to prevent Black from keeping clear. See ISAF Case 15.

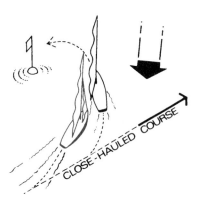

**18.2(c)** Not Overlapped   The course is from a reach to a reach. W luffs head to wind. L cannot get between W and the mark because of Rule 18.2(c). After L has steered to pass under W's stern then W can tack and continue.

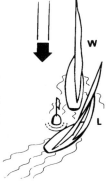

page

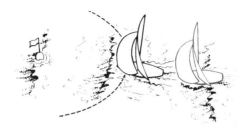

### 18.2(e) Overlap Rights

We all know how boats surge back and forth relative to each other on waves. If there is doubt about an overlap being broken or established just at the moment when the leading boat is within two lengths of the mark, it shall be presumed that the situation is not changed, ie you go back to a situation where there was no doubt. So you could say that the doubt (and the Protest Committee) will go against the boat that claims to have changed the situation, and gained an advantage in the very last moment (unless she has very good witnesses).

Red is surfing on a wave with good speed, Red should not risk trying to establish an inside overlap even if Black was three lengths from the mark, because the doubt will go against Red.

### 18.3(a) Tacking at a Mark

Red tacks within the two length zone. Black is 'fetching' the mark because she can round the mark without any more tacks. Rule 18.3 says that 18.2 does not apply so Red is not entitled to room, furthermore Red is infringing 18.3 (a) by causing Black to sail above close-hauled.

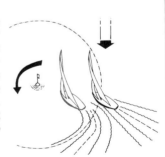

This also applies if the boats were both first on port tack and Black tacked outside the zone without breaking Rule 13 or 15. See ISAF Case 95.

212

If the mark were to be rounded to starboard, Black would not be fetching the mark even if she is on the layline because she would need one more tack to round the mark. Rule 18.3 would NOT apply and the situation would be governed by Rules 11, 15 and 18.2.

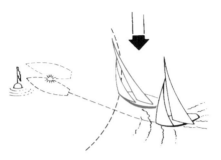

### 18.3(b) Tacking at a Mark

If Red tacks within the two-length zone, Black would have the right of way before the tack, (Rule 10) and during the tack (Rule 13). After the tack, Rule 18.2 does not apply but Black is entitled to room because of Rule 18.3(b). Black becomes overlapped inside Red, so Red shall also keep clear under Rule 11and is not initially protected by Rule 15. If, however, Red completes the tack and Black then luffs after an overlap is established, Rule 16 applies. See ISAF Case 93.

Had Red tacked outside the two-length zone, the situation would have been the same, except that Black would also be entitled to room under Rule 18.2 if there was an overlap when Red entered the two-length zone.

### 18.3(b) Tacking

Red tacks within two lengths of the mark. Black becomes overlapped inside. Red shall keep clear under Rule 18.3(b), so Red cannot deny Black room even if she was first inside the two-length zone.

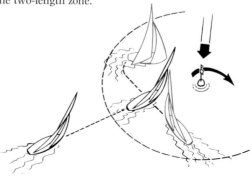

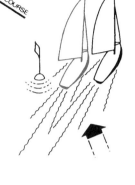

**18.4    Gybing**

Red must gybe on to her proper
course. Black can choose what
she does. This rule takes precedence over Rule 17.1(see preamble Section C), so even if
Red earlier had the right to sail
above her proper course, she
lost that right when they
became about to pass the mark
and Rule 18 started to apply.

**18.4    Gybing**

Red must gybe on to the new proper course at the earliest
opportunity. She is not allowed to continue and force the
others to keep clear even if they are on port tack. Rule 18
applies (see definition Clear Astern etc) and takes precedence
over  Rule 10 because there is conflict. See ISAF Case 75.

213

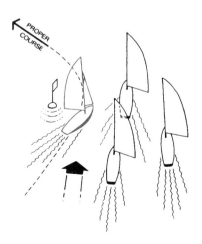

## 18.5 Room at a Continuing Obstruction

This is an awkward Rule to interpret. Presumably the leading boat is already as close to the obstruction as she thinks she can go with safety. Therefore it is difficult for the overtaking boat to show that she can safely go closer.

The two-length limit does not apply, so it is dangerous to try for an overlap under this rule. However if an overlap is established correctly, Black cannot luff Red ashore.

See also ISAF Cases 16, 29 and 33 for further interpretations of this rule.

213
212

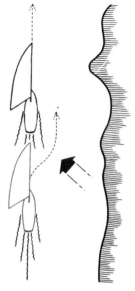

## 18.5 Room at a Continuing Obstruction

Black must be careful when arriving at a break in the obstruction. This is Red's chance to establish an overlap.

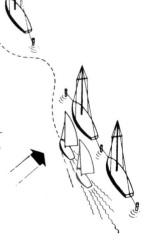

19    **Room to Tack at an Obstruction**

Black can no longer continue in safety, so she hails. Red must tack as soon as possibly after she hears Black's hail. Black must give Red time to respond to the hail and then tack as soon as possible after Red. If Black observes no response to her hail a second hail might be required. See ISAF Case 54.

page

214

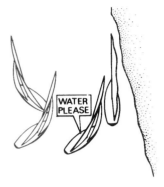

19    **Room to Tack at an Obstruction**

Black has the right to call for water, but Red can reply 'You tack!' and then she is obliged to keep clear of Black. Black must start to tack immediately after Red's reply hail.

Red must remember that in the case of a protest she will have to prove that she has kept clear of Black during this manoeuvre.

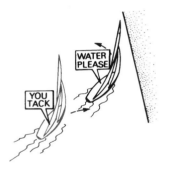

19    **Room to Tack at an Obstruction**

In this case, Red is easily able to tack and keep clear of Black. She has no right to call for water. She only has the right to call for water when she is certain that she cannot clear Black either by passing ahead, or by bearing away under her stern. See ISAF Case 35.

213

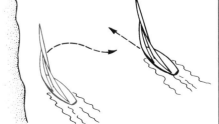

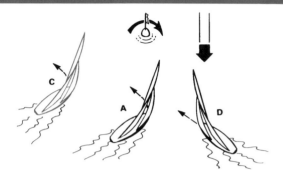

## 19  Room to Tack at an Obstruction

Yacht A can hail C for room to tack, because D is an obstruction to A. Yacht C must tack (or keep clear some other way if possible). It is of no significance whether C can lay the mark or not, because the mark is not the obstruction. Even if it was a port hand rounding, C cannot claim room at the mark from A (Rule 18) because boat D is on starboard and has the right of way over both A and C. The situation is exactly as if the mark was not there. See ISAF Case 3.

## 19  Room to Tack at an Obstruction

Black can hail Red for room to tack, because the boat running is an obstruction that requires her to make a substantial course change.

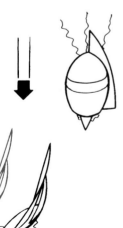

page

**19.2** If Black can fetch the mark, 19.1 does not apply and she need not give Red room to tack.

If Red had been slightly more to windward she would have been able to hail for water to tack under Rule 19 because of the mooring rope which is an obstruction but not part of the mark. See Definitions.

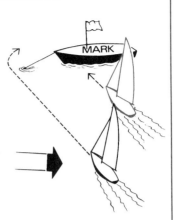

**19.2** **Case 1** The starting line is between two buoys. The starting vessel is not a starting mark but ranks as an obstruction.

In this situation boat D can hail boat C for room to tack at any time. Yacht C can only hail boat A for room to tack because of the starting vessel and not to pass the right side of the starting mark. If boat D were not there, boat C might have been forced to sail over the line between the mark and the starting boat before she could claim room.

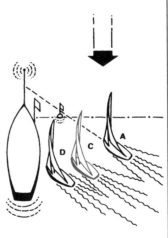

**Case 2** The starting vessel is a starting mark, as is the inner limit mark.

Neither boat D nor boat C can claim room to tack from boat A when the obstruction is a starting mark, and that includes the anchor line.

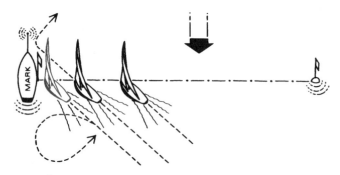

19.2   The starting vessel forms one end of the line and is therefore
       a starting mark. The vessel and the anchor line are also an
       obstruction, so according to 19.2, Red is not entitled to room
       to tack. The middle boat cannot claim room to tack for the
       anchor line according to 19.2; even if the anchor line is not
       part of the mark according to definitions, Rule 18 does also
       not apply at a starting mark or its anchor line so she is not
       entitled to room to pass under Rule 18 even if she could do
       so without tacking. Red only has rights under Rule 11 as if
       the mark was not there.

19.2   In the case of a starting line
       transit which is completely
       on the shore, both before and
       after the start signal, Black
       can hail Red for water to tack
       because not only the starting
       mark but the whole shoreline
       is an obstruction when they
       are approaching to start.

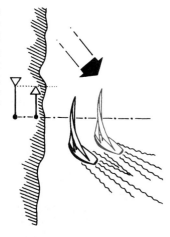

19    After Red has declined Black's hail to tack, the latter bears away in order to tack and pass under Red's stern. Now the wind shifts and Red cannot lay the mark any longer. Because of her refusal, Red has violated Rule 19 and she must take an alternative penalty or retire.

page

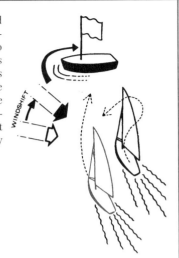

## Section D – Other Rules

20    **Starting Errors**

Even though a boat which has started too early is on starboard tack, she has to keep clear of all others – even port tack boats when she sails towards the pre-start side of the line.

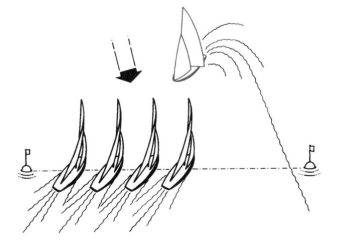

179

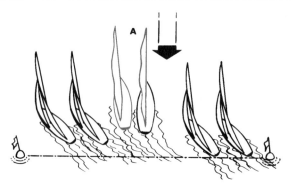

## 20    Starting Errors

Red has started too early and luffs into the wind in order to slow down so that she can drop back and start again. However, she keeps her rights until it is clear that she is sailing a course towards the pre-start side of the starting line. So A has to keep clear as long as Red is still pointing up wind and not sailing backwards. Red could be luffing to protect herself and not because she was early in the start.

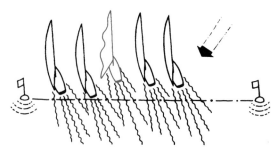

## 20    Starting Errors

The Red boat has started too early but the only thing she can do is let the jib and the mainsail go. She can slow down by backing the sails if she is able without affecting the leeward boat (which has right of way), and without moving astern. As soon as it is clear that she is not making her way up the course and she has begun to decrease the distance to the startline she has begun her manoeuvre of 'sailing towards the pre-start side of the starting line', and she must keep clear of other boats.

**20    Starting Errors**

As soon as the starting signal is made, the Red boats, who are on the wrong side of the line, must keep clear. After the starting signal they have no right-of-way because they have to comply with Rule 29.1 (returning to start). If Rule 30.1 (round the ends) applies, they already lose right of way during the last minute before the signal.

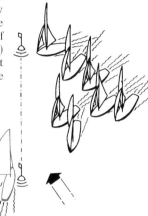

**20    Starting Errors and**
**15    Acquiring Right of Way**

Even though she has regained her starboard tack rights when she is completely on the pre-start side of the line, the Red boat must now initially give boat A room to keep clear under Rule 15. It will be impossible for boat A to comply in this situation.

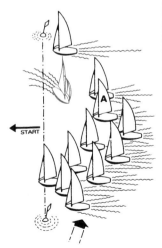

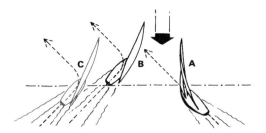

20 **Starting Errors**

Yacht B has started too early and, because of the starboard tack boat, she has to call upon boat C for room to tack. Yacht B has the right to do this because she is not yet sailing towards the pre-start side of the starting line. After tacking she can then begin to slow down.

20 **Penalty Turns**

If you are exonerating yourself after touching a mark, or are taking a 720° turn penalty, you are on a proper course all the time. However you must keep clear of non-penalised boats when you are making the turn, ie from when you start the turn till you are back on the course where you started your turn.

20 **Moving Astern**

A and B are on starboard tack, but they are early in the start. They start moving astern by deliberately backing the main. As long as they are moving ahead or still in the water A has right of way over C -starboard (Rule 10), B has right over D-leeward (Rule 11) and E-clear ahead (Rule 12), but as soon as they start moving astern by backing the main they become give-way boats. When Rule 20 applies, the rules of Section A do not, according to the preamble of Section D. A boat that goes

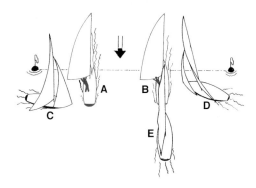

head to wind with flapping sails and stops, maybe even drifting somewhat astern, does *not* lose her rights. Only moving astern *by backing a sail* comes under Rule 20.

page

21 **Capsized Dinghy**
You have to keep clear of a capsized dinghy until she has regained control. Under the Rules it is the same as if it was an obstruction.

## Hailing situations summarised

1 **Obligatory hailing situations**

(a) Hail for room to tack at an obstruction (Rule 19).

(b) A protesting boat shall try to inform another boat that she intends to protest. Hailing is mandatory if it is an incident in the racing area and the protested boat is within hailing distance (61.1 a).

2 **Recommended hailing situations**

(a) Any situation or manoeuvre where a hail would clarify or support one's case, eg in the establishment or termination of an overlap at a mark or obstruction (Rule 18) or in a luffing situation (Rule 17.1).

(b) If a boat needs to be avoided because she is out of control, aground or helping someone in the water (Rule 21) a hail could be relevant to warn other boats.

(c) To avoid a collision, a right-of-way boat may hail before she makes an alteration of course that may not be foreseen by another boat (Rule 16).

# PART 3 – CONDUCT OF A RACE

**25**    **Race Signals**

In a recall situation, where no sound signal is given, there can be no recall. Race signals must be accompanied by a sound signal when indicated in 'Race Signals'. See ISAF Cases 31 and 71.

**25**    **Race Signals**

Always be prepared so that you can recognise signals, in case the Committee stops the race at one of the marks, shortens the course in a special way, or changes a mark as provided in the Sailing Instructions. See the back cover of this book for quick reference.

**26.1**    **Starting Systems**

Note the timing of the start shall be governed by the *visual starting signal*. The timing is made from the flag/shape and not from the gun, bell, whistle or hooter. Even if the sound signal is not made at all, the failure shall be disregarded.

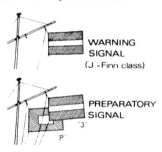

WARNING SIGNAL
(J´=Finn class)

PREPARATORY SIGNAL

**28.1**    **Sailing the Course and**
**30.1**    **I Flag Rule**

During a normal start, a boat which is over the line early can re-start like boat D. However, if the 'round-the-ends' Rule 30.1 is invoked ( Code flag I was flown), as frequently happens after a general recall, then a boat which is over the line will have to return like boat A.

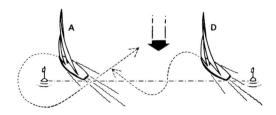

28.1

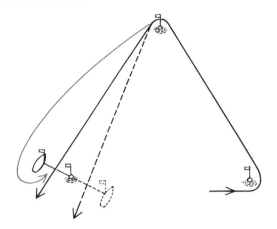

page

**Sailing the Course and Definitions**
If the Sailing Instructions say that you should finish by leaving the Committee boat to port and, for example, they put the Committee boat on the wrong side of the mark, you should follow the finishing definition of the Rules exactly (in the direction from the last mark), even if you thereby leave the Committee boat to starboard and thus violate the Sailing Instructions. See ISAF Cases 45 and 82.

200

28.1 **Sailing the Course**
Red has rounded incorrectly. Black is right. You have to unwind yourself before rounding properly.

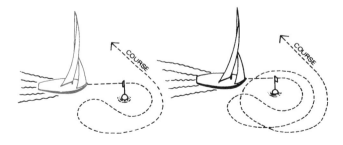

page

**28.2** **Required Side of Mark**

The course is: Start, mark 1, mark 2, mark 3 etc. Both marks 1 and 2 are marks of the course for boat A.

B has just rounded mark 2 and therefore mark 1 is no longer considered as a mark for her.

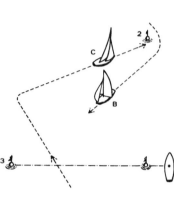

C has not yet rounded mark 1 and therefore she can please herself which side of mark 2 she goes. She can touch it without infringing. See also Rule 31.1 and ISAF Case 58.

215

**28.1&**
**28.2** **Sailing the Course**

A starting mark has a 'required side' when a boat approaches to start, but it must not be touched before the start (Rule 31.1).

Black must be correct because she has passed the limit mark on the required side when approaching the line to start.

Red is wrong because the mark had already been passed before she was 'approaching the starting line from its pre-start side to start'. For a further interpretation of the 'string' rule see ISAF Case 90.

215

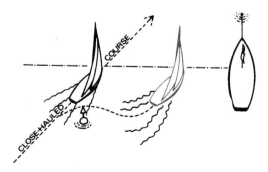

page

28    **Sailing the Course and**
      **Definitions: Finishing and Racing**
      Red, who has crossed the finishing
      line, still has to keep clear of the star-
      board tack boats as she is still racing.
      She can go under their sterns and
      still maintain her finishing position
      because she has already finished. She
      may clear the line in any direction.

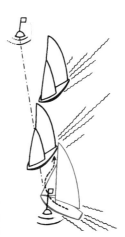

29    **Starting; Recalls**
      The method of recall is made clear in
      this rule. The onus is on the boat to
      see that it not only starts correctly
      (see also Rule 28) but also returns
      correctly if it is over the line at the
      starting signal. There is no provision
      in the rules for the Committee to try to inform the individual
      boats any further, by individual hail or likewise. This might even
      be unfair, as the boats that are informed first can return to start       215
      earlier than the boats that are informed later. ISAF Cases 31, 71         216
      and 79 contains further interpretations of this rule.

30.3  **Black Flag Rule**
      Even if a boat believes that the Race Committee has made an
      error in disqualifying her under this rule and intends to
      claim redress, she is not entitled to sail in the next race. This
      is a bit sad because if she is right and is granted redress it is
      more difficult for the Race Committee to give a fair redress        216
      when the boat has not sailed the race. See ISAF Case 96.

31.1  **Touching a Mark and**
      **Definition: Mark**
      You can touch the buoy rope
      with the keel without infring-
      ing Rule 31.1. If you foul the
      rope and it is caught round
      the keel or rudder you can
      use your own gear to clear it.

# Rule 31

**31.1   Touching a Mark and
Definition: Mark**
You can touch the dinghy
tied up at the stern of the
start vessel, even if the
vessel ranks as a mark.
The dinghy is only attached temporarily.

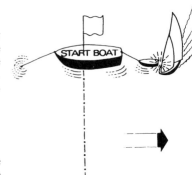

**31     Touching a Mark**
Once you have hit the
mark you must do one
of three things. Either:

(a)   exonerate yourself under Rule 31.2 (one complete 360°
      turn)
(b)   protest another boat involved in the incident under Rule
      60 (the other boat can accept a 720° turn penalty or
      risk being disqualified later), or
(c)   exonerate yourself by accepting a 720° turn penalty if
      you think that besides touching the mark you also
      broke a rule yourself. See ISAF Case 56.

216

Contact with a mark by a boat's equipment constitutes

200     touching it, See ISAF Case 77, but you do not necessarily
        break Rule 31 if you touch a mark that shifts as a result of

216     another boat touching it. See ISAF Case 28.

**31     Touching a Mark**
If you hit a starting mark while racing, ie after the preparatory
signal, you must complete your exoneration as soon as possible
(it might be before the starting signal except for a match race).
If you hit a finishing mark you must complete your exoneration before you finish again. See also Definitions: Racing and
Finishing.

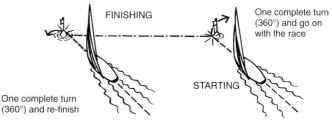

FINISHING

One complete turn
(360°) and go on
with the race

STARTING

One complete turn
(360°) and re-finish

**31     Touching a Finishing
       Mark**

According to the defi-
nition of racing and
Rule 31, if this boat
touches the mark,
even after she has
crossed the finishing
line, she must exon-
erate herself and does
not finish until she
crosses the line a sec-
ond time.

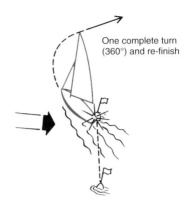

One complete turn
(360°) and re-finish

**31     Touching a Mark**

After touching the mark, both these tracks will correct the
error. The key to what has to be done is:

1   Sail clear of the other boats as soon as possible.
2   Promptly do one complete 360° turn which must
    include one tack and one gybe; keep clear of other boats
    while turning, and be sure you end up on the same
    course as when you started the 360° turn.
3   Ensure the mark has been rounded correctly according
    to Rule 28.1.

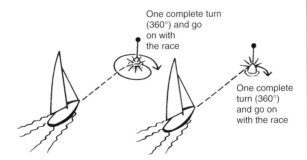

One complete turn
(360°) and go
on with
the race

One complete
turn (360°)
and go on
with the race

**32     Shortening or Abandoning After the Start**

When a race is abandoned after only a few boats finishing,
their results stand and the Race Committee must consider
redress to the boats that were still racing. See also ISAF Case
37 when abandoning races in a multi-class regatta.

216

page

# PART 4 – OTHER REQUIREMENTS WHEN RACING

**41** **Outside Help**

Except for in-team racing a boat is not allowed to receive outside help. There was a case where it was suspected that a crew was using a walkie-talkie radio to contact someone on shore. If it had been proved, then the boat would have been disqualified.

**41**
**47.2** **Outside Help and Limitations on Crew**

If a boat loses a man overboard, she may receive help or assistance from another competitor or spectator boat as long as no forward progress is made during the recovery operation.

**42** **Propulsion**

217

ISAF Cases 5, 8 and 69 contains interpretations of this rule.

**43** **Competitor Clothing and Appendix J**

In the third paragraph of Appendix J, a competitor whose weight of wet clothing and equipment exceeds the amount permitted may rearrange the clothing and equipment on the draining rack and repeat the test. This may be interpreted as reweighing the clothing and equipment piece by piece. Drinking containers like 'camelbacks ' must not be worn while racing. See ISAF Case 89.

217

**45** **Anchoring and Definition: Starting**

A boat may anchor after her preparatory signal, but here Red has a part of her equipment on the wrong side of the line at the starting signal, so Red has not started correctly.

page

## 47.2    Limitations on Crew

When capsizing near the
finishing line, a boat may
finish with crew members
in the water provided they
have physical contact with
the boat.

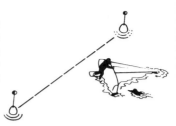

## 49    Crew Position

Crews racing in off-shore
boats equipped with upper
and lower lifelines of wire
(not rope), are permitted to
have their bodies outside
the upper lifeline when sitting on the deck facing
outboard. See also ISAF
Case Book, Case 36 for
illustrations of crew posi-
tioning relative to lifelines.
Case 83 contains further
interpretations of this rule.

217

## 50.3    Use of Outriggers

Be careful how you fix your jib fairleads so that they do not
contravene this Rule, but a hand holding out a sheet is not
an outrigger, as it is not a
'fitting'. See ISAF Case 4.

217

The spinnaker sheet may
be led over the main boom
or through a block on the
main boom. A guy is not a
sheet so a jockey pole
attached to a spinnaker
guy is not an outrigger.
See ISAF Case 97.

217

## 51    Movable Ballast

Items of the boat's gear shall not be moved about the boat.
Unless in use, gear must remain in its designated place.

## PART 5 – PROTESTS, HEARINGS, MISCONDUCT AND APPEALS

**60   Right to Protest**

The responsibility for protesting, primarily rests with the competitors. The Race Committee is not burdened to know and enforce the class rules when the members of the class themselves fail to do so. See ISAF Cases 39 and 68.

218

218

ISAF Case 1, 42 and 80 also refers to right to protest.

**61.1(a)   Informing the Protestee, Protest flag**

219

The flag must be flown at the first reasonable opportunity following an incident. See ISAF Case 72 for interpretation of the word flag. A protest is not lodged until it is written on paper and handed to the Race Committee. Do not be afraid to fly the protest flag if you are in any doubt. You may find when you get ashore that it is not necessary to continue with the protest, in which case you do not have to lodge it.

**61.1(a)   Informing the Protestee**

218

A protesting boat must attempt to inform the protested boat but it is not mandatory that she succeeds in the attempt. However, you must convince the Protest Committee of your attempts. See ISAF Case 42.

**61.2   Contents**

219

A protest shall be in writing. A boat that is involved in an infringement, but which she believes is not her fault must nevertheless lodge a written protest if she wishes to clear herself. Citing the correct rule to have been broken is not necessary. See ISAF Case 22,

**62   Redress**

219

The Race Committee cannot be protested by a boat or a competitor. Instead the boat may seek redress only when she alleges that her finishing position has been significantly worse by a fault made by the Race Committee and through no fault of her own. See ISAF Case 44.

**63.2    Time and place of hearing**                                   page

All information necessary for the competitors shall be available to them but they shall make an effort to obtain the
information. See ISAF Case 48.                                          219

**64.1    Penalties and Exoneration**

Boat B on starboard was hit by boat C on port(1), and
knocked on to the other tack. Boat B was now nearly stopped
on port tack and was hit by boat D who was on starboard (2).
Boat B is not wrong because she was compelled by C to break
Rule 10. She should Protest boat C, and be exonerated. In a
protest arising from contact the Committee must find facts
and give a decision on them. See also ISAF Case 10.                     219

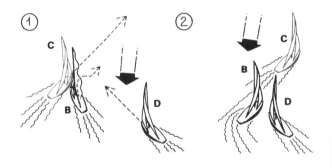

Separate protests in closely connected incidents should be
heard together. See ISAF Case 49.                                      220

**70      Right of Appeal**

A boat may appeal only if she has been party to the protest. If she
was not party to the protest, but was affected by the decision she
must seek redress under the terms of Rule 62. See ISAF Case 55.        221

# PART 6 – ENTRY AND QUALIFICATION

78    **Certificates**

With increasing regularity there are protests concerning these certificates. Owners must satisfy Rule 78.1 in making sure that their boat complies with the certificates issued to them. Provided this is satisfied then they cannot be retrospectively invalidated after a race or series is completed. See ISAF Case 57 for interpretation of Rule 78.3.

# PART 7 – RACE ORGANISATION

page

86      **Rules Changes**
87      **Notice of Race**
88      **Sailing Instructions**
        Many clubs do not take enough trouble over the Notice of Race
        and Sailing Instructions. This often results in confusion, disap-
        pointment and bad feelings. It is really very simple for clubs to
        go through Rules 87, 88 and Appendix M and N and make out
        standard forms which can cover almost all races. Rule 86 speci-
        fies that the Sailing Instructions shall not alter some specified
        Rules. However other rules can be changed by referring specifi-
        cally to the Rule and stating the change. Note class rules may
        not alter a racing rule unless the alteration is permitted by the
        racing rule itself (ISAF Case 85). Committees should be careful          222
        not to say and change too much. It is highly recommended
        that the organisers use the standard Sailing Instructions wher-
        ever possible, so that the competitors do not have to learn a
        whole new 'book' of Sailing Instructions for every event they go
        to. It should be a sailing contest not a reading contest.

88      **Sailing Instructions**
        The drawing illustrates some of the problems for Race
        Committees and shows the likely situation when the windward
        mark is rounded to port. The disadvantage of port rounding is
        that a boat approaching on port tack, even though she may
        really be leading as Red is here, may not be able to round the
        mark, and can drop many places. Also the tendency is to use
        only the starboard side of the course.

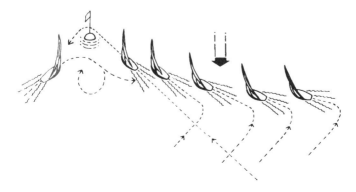

**88      Sailing Instructions**

With starboard rounding, a boat can always get round the
mark by standing on a few lengths, but there are usually
more protest situations.

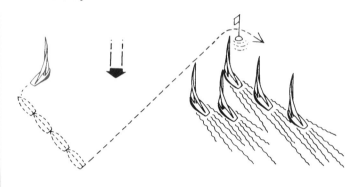

**88.2(c)  Changes to Sailing Instructions**

Unless there is a special procedure laid down in the Sailing
Instructions, they cannot be changed unless by written
amendment. Oral instructions can easily be misunderstood
or even forgotten. See ISAF Case 32.

# APPENDIX C – MATCH RACING
# RULES

page

16    In match racing it is common for the right-of-way boat to alter
      course and 'hunt' the give way boat while she is trying to keep
      clear. This is to gain a 'controlling' position , and she can do
      this without breaking Rule 16 as long as the give-way boat
      still has at least one opportunity to keep clear. A typical exam-
      ple is when the boats first meet after entering the starting area.

      In the situation below, A luffs slowly to give way when there
      is still some distance between the boats. B responds by also
      luffing, maintaining a collision course 'hunting' A. A has no
      choice but to luff further and eventually to tack as the last pos-
      sibility to keep clear. B now has a controlling position and can
      'take' A to the left side of the course, the 'Red zone'. B will
      probably win the start.

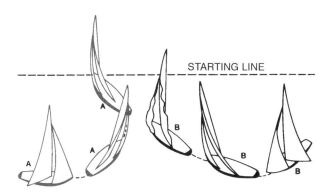

In the second situation D keeps bearing away until the boats are very close. Her only possibility to keep clear is then to luff hard. E can no longer 'hunt' because of Rule 16. She must let D pass to windward and cannot force her to tack. Instead the boats will probably go into a circling manoeuvre.

It is more risky for the port tack boat to meet on opposite tacks in the pre-start when the boats are closer to the wind because it is easier for the starboard tack boat to gain a controlling position.

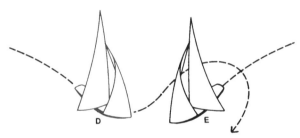

STARTING LINE

**Umpired matches**

When umpires are employed in match racing there will usually be one umpire boat with two umpires to each match. Each umpire will 'adopt' one boat. The umpire plays the role of 'his' boat and constantly states what she is doing, who is give-way boat and why. Thus the umpires 'discuss' the situation as it develops and often will have decided the infringement as it occurs. Let us follow the typical luffing situation in the pre-start manoeuvre shown opposite.

A establishes an overlap from clear astern and luffs. A's umpire will follow if B was given room initially (Rule 15) and if A is luffing according to Rule 16. B's umpire will follow if B takes action to keep clear under Rule 11 and the definition of Keep Clear when A gets the overlap. The umpires also have to observe if the overlap is broken. When the collision occurs, the umpires have already in the left situation agreed that: (1) The overlap was not established too close and (2) A luffed slowly giving B room to keep clear (3) B did not take sufficient action to keep clear and establish a 'safety distance' from A and

page

finally (4) B is through head to wind, ie she has tacked. All these circumstances put together amount to a penalty for B.

In the situation on the right, which is not very different and probably the way B saw the first situation, (1) D is establishing the overlap too close to E, not initially giving room for E to keep clear and (2) E has made a reasonable effort to try to keep clear. Penalty awarded to D.

It is obvious that there are other situations similar to these two where the decisions are not so clearcut. Competitors must remember that in match racing they do not have the opportunity to take their case to a jury. They must rely on the umpires' knowledge of the rules and their ability to follow the manoeuvres. In very complicated situations involving several rules, the umpires' view of the situation may be very different from that of the competitor. They should not risk a close situation when the decision can go either way. It is safer to try to 'give' the other boat a penalty in situations where the rights and obligations are more obvious and the worst you risk is a 'green flag'.

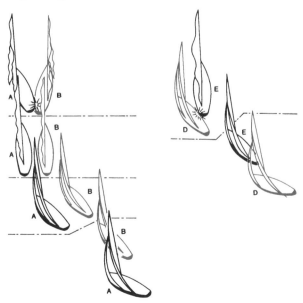

# ISAF INTERPRETATIONS
## OF THE
# RACING RULES

## Definitions

**Finishing**

*ISAF Case 45.* The finishing definition cannot be overruled by a Sailing Instruction. The Protest Committee is not entitled to grant redress so as to negate the definition of finishing.

**Finishing**

*ISAF Case 82.* When a finishing line is laid so closely in line with the last leg that it cannot be determined which is the correct way to cross it in order to finish in accordance with the definition, competitors are eligible for redress, and either direction is acceptable.

**Keep Clear**

*ISAF Case 77.* Contact with a mark by a boat's equipment constitutes touching it. The fact that she touches because she has manoeuvring or sail-handling difficulties does not excuse her infringement. A boat obligated to keep clear does not break a rule when touched by a right-of-way boat's equipment that has moved out of normal position. See however Case 91 below.

**Keep Clear**

*ISAF Case 91.* A boat required to keep clear of another boat's equipment out of its normal position when the equipment has been out of its normal position long enough  for the equipment to have been seen. See Case 77 above.

**Obstruction**

*ISAF Case 41.* W (to windward) and L (to leeward), who are overlapped, are overtaking A (ahead), all on the same tack. A ranks as an obstruction to W and L. When they 'are about to pass', Rule 18.2(a) starts to apply.W or L can elect to pass their respective sides of A under 18.2(a) and must allow room to the boat that becomes inside overlapped. The inside boat is not required to hail for room, but it would be prudent to hail to avoid misunderstandings.

**Proper Course**

> *ISAF Case 14.* There can be more than one 'proper course'. Which of two different courses is the faster one cannot be determined in advance, and is not necessarily proven by one boat or the other reaching the next mark ahead. When, owing to a difference of opinion as to proper course, two boats on the same tack converge, the windward boat must keep clear.

**Proper Course**

> *ISAF Case 46* refers to two boats on converging courses approaching the finishing line. In the absence of W, L would have luffed to finish at right angles to the line, but W wished to sail dead down wind to finish at the starboard end of the finishing line. L did not have the right to sail above proper course. However Rule 11 says that when two boats on the same tack overlap then the windward boat shall keep clear, even if L is limited by Rules 16 and 17.1. From the evidence it seemed that L's proper course was correct, and provided that she fulfilled Rule 16, she could sail up to her proper course.

**Rules**

> *ISAF Case 98.* The Rules included in the definition apply whether or not the NoR or SI so state, except the prescriptions of a national authority and Appendix A-Scoring, which apply only when so stated in the NoR or SI. The rules of a handicapping or rating system are 'class rules' and therefore apply when a boat races under them. Rules M1.2(8) and M2.2(5) do not permit an organizing authority or race committee to make changes to class rules unless the class rules themselves permit such changes.

# Sportsmanship and the Rules

> *ISAF Case 65.* A boat knows she has infringed the black flag rule, but continues to race in order to hinder a rival competitor. Under the principles of sportsmanship she is obliged to retire promptly. She is found to have committed a gross breach of good sportsmanship and therefore has broken Rule 2. She is excluded not only from that race, but from the series under Rule 69.1.

# PART 1 – FUNDAMENTAL RULES

RULE NO

1.1     *ISAF Case 20.* Helping those in danger. Rendering assistance to those in danger is compulsory to those in a position to do so. It does not matter that help may not have been asked for, nor that subsequently it may be shown not to have been needed. So a boat rendering assistance may be entitled to redress.

2     *ISAF Case 47. Fair Sailing.* A boat that deliberately hails 'Starboard', when she is on port tack, has not acted fairly, and is therefore liable to disqualification under Rule 2.

2     *ISAF Case 73.* W and L were overlapped. The crew of L deliberately touched W's deck with a hand and intimated that W should retire. W was disqualified but appealed successfully. When, by deliberate action, L's crew touches W, which action could have no other intention than to cause W to break Rule 11, then L breaks Rule 2.

2     *ISAF Case 74.* There is no rule that dictates how the helmsman or crew of a leeward boat must sit. Contact with a windward boat does not break Rule 2 unless either the helmsman's or crew's position is deliberately misused. In this case there was no indication of deliberate misuse from the leeward boat. See also Case 73 above.

2     *ISAF Case 78.* On a finish leg of the final race of a series, boat A suddenly sails back towards B and positions herself in a tactically controlling position over B. Three boats passed them so A would defeat B in the series. This tactic of making it difficult for B did not break Rule 2 because A broke no other rule and only intended to benefit her series score.

# PART 2 – WHEN BOATS MEET

**Preamble**

> *ISAF Case 38. Sailing Instruction content.* Between sunset and sunrise the International Regulations for Prevention of Collisions at Sea (IRPCS) might replace the ISAF rules. The IRPCS are intended to ensure the safety of vessels at sea by precluding situations that might lead to collisions. They effectively prohibit a right-of-way boat from changing course (eg luffing) when she is close to a boat obligated to keep clear.

**Preamble**

> *ISAF Case 67.* When a boat that is racing meets a vessel that is not racing, the Government right-of-way rules for the area concerned (usually the IRPCS rules) apply. In this case the racing boat is the give-way boat, but deliberately rams the cruising boat. Not only has she infringed the preamble of Part 2 which obliges her to comply with the Government right-of-way rules but also she was penalised for gross misconduct under Rule 69.

## Section A – Right of Way

RULE NO

10   *ISAF Case 50.* In a straightforward port and starboard case, a Protest Committee must inquire carefully into whether the starboard tack boat did actually bear away to avoid collision, or that there was genuine and reasonable apprehension of collision. If this was so, then the port tack boat should be disqualified.

RULE NO

10    **ISAF Case 23.** *Opposite tacks versus Rule 18 Passing Marks.* W and L were running on port tack. S overtakes first L and then W and sails between them. S has right-of-way under Rule 10 over both port tack boats; consequently W does not rank as an obstruction to S and Rule 18.2(a) does not apply between S and L.

10    **ISAF Case 88.** S (starboard boat) and P (port boat) approached each other on a windward leg. When three lengths away, S hailed 'starboard' and again at two lengths. P did not respond. S, fearing collision luffed sharply and P bore away. Seeing this, S bore away also to swing her transom away and P passed astern of S within two feet. P was disqualified for not keeping clear. A boat may avoid contact and yet fail to keep clear.

10    **ISAF Case 43.** *Approaching a continuing obstruction on opposite tacks.* P was sailing close-hauled close to, and parallel with, a continuing obstruction. S approached on a collision course after completing a tack. As P had the time she should have kept clear of S after S tacked on to starboard and approached on a collision course.

11    **ISAF Case 13.** *Same tack overlapped before starting.* A boat does not break Rule 16 when holding a steady converging close-hauled course toward a windward boat even if she luffed before she came on converging course. Rule 11 applies; W must keep clear even if this means she is over the line early.

RULE NO

11   *ISAF Case 51.* This is a situation where there are intervening windward boats being prevented from luffing clear of a leeward boat and forced into breaking Rule 11 solely because of the most windward boat's failure to keep clear. The Protest Committee must exonerate boats when they are compelled by another to break a rule.

11   *ISAF Case 25. On the same tack and Rule 18.2(a) Passing Marks.* W and L were passing a leeward mark. L gave W adequate room but W was slow in rounding the mark and sheeting in so her boom hit L. The Protest Committee found as a fact that W did not round the mark on to a proper course as soon as she had room to do so and there was contact. It was clear that W and L had passed the mark and that there was no reason for W to sail below her proper course. Rule 18.2(a) had ceased to apply; basic Rule 11 applied. W was disqualified.

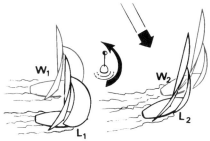

13   *ISAF Case 17. While tacking.* A boat has to keep clear under Rule 13 until she is heading on a close-hauled course, regardless of her movement through the water, or the sheeting of her sails.

## Section B – General Limitations

14   *ISAF Case 26. Avoiding Contact.* Two boats in different races were rounding the same mark in opposite directions. Rule 10 applied; P was disqualified. S claimed that had she changed course she would have broken Rule 16, but S was  disqualified for failing to avoid a collision which resulted in damage. Rule 14 overrides Rule 16 when a collision likely to cause damage is imminent.

14   *ISAF Case 87.* In a start, a starboard tack close-hauled boat S was struck amidships at right angles by a port tack boat. Realising the imminent collision, S altered course in the last moment but there was considerable damage. S was not disqualified under Rule 14. A right-of-way boat need not anticipate that the other boat will not keep clear.

# ISAF Interpretations

RULE NO

**14(b)** *ISAF Case 19. Avoiding contact, interpretation of 'damage'.* In considering whether damage occurred, the following is suggested to be considered. Was the value of the boat, or part of the boat, diminished? Was anything made less functional? Was a member of the crew injured?

**15** *ISAF Case 27. Acquiring right of way.* A leeward boat L on port tack tacked on the starboard lay line and W had no time to avoid a collision. The Protest Committee disqualified L under Rule 15 but also disqualified W, pointing out that she knew that L was going to tack but did nothing to avoid collision. W appealed successfully. A boat is not required to anticipate that another boat will infringe a rule. A newly obligated boat is entitled to time for response.

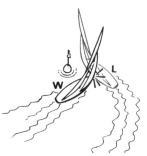

**15** *ISAF Case 24.* When A establishes a leeward overlap on B from clear astern, Rule 12 ceases to apply. B then becomes bound by Rule 11, A by Rule 15. The phrase 'room to keep clear' in Rule 15 means that A, in order to fulfil her obligation under Rule 11, must keep clear as best she can and, if this requires her to luff, she must do so. If this causes her to touch B, B has not given A enough room to keep clear. However, a clearly unnecessary or excessive luff by A causing contact with B infringes Rule 11. But B's obligation under Rule 15 is not a continuing one. If A fails to respond promptly after the overlap begins, B is no longer obligated.

**15** *ISAF Case 7. Overtaking to leeward.* When running towards a mark, L steered a course to overtake W and pass to leeward. The moment L established an overlap, W became subject to Rule 11. L at the same time became bound by Rule 15 and had to allow W room to keep clear. This obligation, however, is not continuative. L was also subject to Rule 17.1 and could not sail above her proper course. In this case, when approaching the mark, L luffed slightly and touched W. It was established that the luff was justified as being an alteration to a new proper course and W was therefore wrong under Rule 11.

**15** *ISAF Case 53.* Thirty seconds before a start W was dead in the water with sails flapping. L, approaching from leeward, hailed 'Leeward boat' before an overlap was established. L then had to bear away immediately when she established an overlap. W took no evasive action until after L had established an overlap. No contact was made. W, being clear ahead need not anticipate her obligation to keep clear before being overlapped to leeward from clear astern. Neither boat was penalised as no rule was infringed.

RULE NO

**16**     *ISAF Case 6. Changing course.* When sailing to windward, P bore away to pass astern of S. S, however, tacked. P resumed her course after S had come on port tack close-hauled. There was no collision. In this case Rules 13 and 16 were complied with so no one was at fault. A starboard-tack boat that tacks after a port-tack boat has borne away to go astern of her is not necessarily breaking a rule.

**16**     *ISAF Case 92.* S and P were approaching on a beat on opposite tacks in strong winds. When P bore away to keep clear S also bore away to 'hunt'. P bore away further but because of S heeling the rigs collided when the boats passed on opposite tacks. S was disqualified under Rules 16 and 14. When a right of way boat changes course the keep-clear boat is required to act only in response to what the right-of-way boat is doing at the time, not what she might subsequently do.

**16**     *ISAF Case 52.* Rule 16 does not restrict the course of a keep-clear boat. In a typical match racing pre-start manoeuvre, one boat drives another away from the starting line. Boats A and B reached away from the starting line on port tack. A, moving faster, passed B and became clear ahead. As A luffed to tack so B luffed with her, preventing A from tacking. A then bore away to gybe but B bore away to leeward of her and prevented her from gybing. Rule 16 applies only to a right-of-way boat which B was not, either in position 3 or 4. In position 4, boat B clear astern had to keep clear under Rule 12 and A could not tack without infringing 13. At position 5, B was leeward boat and then held rights under Rule 11.

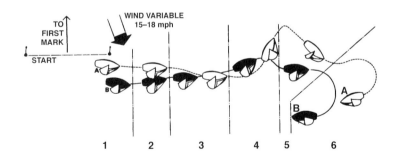

16     *ISAF Case 60. Right of way boat changing course.* Port tack boat A rounded the windward mark to starboard and immediately gybed on to starboard. She decided, for tactical reasons, to reach high above it. As she luffed to her new course she came bow to bow with boat B on port tack still making for the mark. B bore away fast but it was not sufficient and A had to luff sharply as well to avoid a collision. There was no contact. A had no right to luff abruptly into the path of B for whatever reason. Tactical objectives do not relieve a boat of her obligations under the rules. A potentially serious situation occurred and only their combined efforts narrowly averted a collision. A was disqualified for infringing Rule 16.

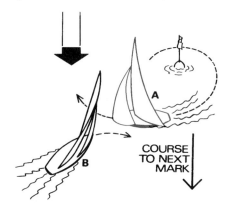

COURSE TO NEXT MARK

16     *ISAF Case 76.* S and P are beating to the finishing line. S has overstood and sails free to round the Committee boat at the starboard end. P can cross S clear ahead until S luffs round the Committee boat when the boats are less than two lengths apart. Rule 18.2(a) does not apply (opposite tacks on a beat to windward). P must keep clear under Rule 10 but S's luff prevents her from keeping clear so S breaks Rule 16.

## Section C – At Marks and Obstructions

18     *ISAF Case 70.* L and W were sailing on starboard tack overlapped approaching a windward starboard mark. W requested room and L replied ' Room will be given when needed'. One and a half lengths from the mark, the boats made contact: beam to beam. W was disqualified under Rule 11. A boat entitled to room under Rule 18 is relieved of her obligations under Rule 11 only to the extent that Rule 18 explicitly provides rights in conflict with Rule 11 and only when room as defined is being denied her.

RULE NO

**18.1**   *ISAF Case 84. When is a boat 'about to pass'?* Almost always; a boat two hull lengths from the mark is about to pass it, but this is sometimes so at a greater distance too. Beside distance, other factors such as boat's speed, wind conditions, current and the amount of sail handling required before or during the rounding may also be relevant.

**18.1**   *ISAF Case 94.* Three dinghies are about to round about four lengths from the mark and start to drop spinnakers. The overlap relationship then changes between them before they reach the two-length zone. Rule 18 begins to apply when boats are about to pass; the distance may vary depending on conditions. See Case 84 above. However, the obligations between boats may still change before the two-length zone. It is only at the zone that it can be determined whether 18.2(b) or 18.2(c) will govern the rounding.

**18.1(b)**   *ISAF Case 9.* Two close-hauled boats meet at a starboard-hand windward mark. S has room to tack and round the mark but holds her course past the mark and forces P to tack. Rule 10 applies, not Rule 18 (opposite tacks on a beat to windward). There is no rule that requires a boat to sail a proper course.

**18.2(a)**   *ISAF Case 12. Overlap on widely differing courses.* OL, on starboard tack, approached a starboard-hand mark close-hauled. IW approached from almost directly upwind and called for room to round the mark inside OL. At the proper time IW had an overlap on OL under the definition and was therefore entitled to room under Rule 18.2(a).

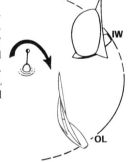

**18**   *ISAF Case 21. An interpretation of room.* 'Room' means enough space needed by an inside boat without right-of-way, which, in the existing conditions is handled in a seamanlike manner, to pass in safety between the object and the outside boat.

**18.2(a)**   *ISAF Case 11.* W and L, overlapping and close-hauled on port tack approaches S, close-hauled on starboard tack. S is an obstruction. Normally W must tack if L calls. But in this case S was not an obstruction to L so L could not ask W to tack under Rule 19.1. W can ask L for room if L chooses to bear away to pass astern of S.

**18.2(a)** *ISAF Case 59.* Four boats in line abreast are running towards a mark on starboard. A fifth boat B is just clear astern of the line of four. The two inside boats A1 and A2 gybe on to port and round the mark satisfactorily. When A3 and A4 change course to gybe and round the mark, they are still outside the two-length circle. This results in B becoming overlapped inside them before they enter the circle. They are able to give B room to round inside. By Rule 18.2(a) B is entitled to room to round the mark inside.

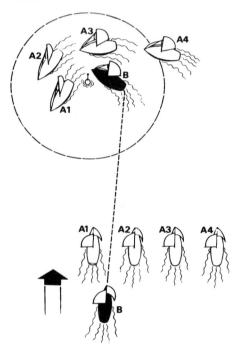

**18.2(a)** *ISAF Case 86.* Boats I (inside) and O (outside) were on port tack overlapped at three lengths from a leeward port-hand mark. At two lengths both gybed. One and a half lengths from the mark I luffed and touched O; no damage occurred. Both then bore away, gybed and rounded the mark closely. I was disqualified but appealed successfully. There was nothing in the facts found or the endorsed diagram that indicated that I had luffed above proper course. When Rules 18.2(a) and 18.4 apply at a leeward mark, an outside windward boat must keep sufficiently clear of the leeward boat so that she is able to sail her proper course while passing the mark.

RULE NO

**18.2(c)** *ISAF Case 2. Not overlapped at mark.* Boat O gybed from port to starboard when abreast of a starboard hand mark but several lengths from it. The inside boat I was on port tack, but clear astern just before O's gybe, but was within two lengths of the mark. O now had to keep clear of I, even when I gybed and became clear ahead of O during the rounding. Rule 18.2(c) did not apply in situation 1 as O was outside the two-lengths zone and not 'about to pass'. After O gybed she had to give I room under Rule 18.2(a).

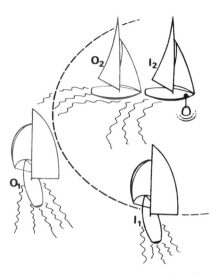

**18.2(a)** *ISAF Case 30.* Two boats A and B are running on the same starboard tack alongside a continuing obstruction, A clear ahead of B. A gybe to port by A does not relieve B of her obligation to keep clear. Rule 18.2(a) applies throughout the incident since they are passing an obstruction on the same side.

**18.2(c)** *ISAF Case 15.* Approaching a windward mark close-hauled, A is clear ahead but to leeward of B. A cannot tack if she thereby infringes Rule 13. B, however can prevent A from tacking but must keep clear if A luffs.

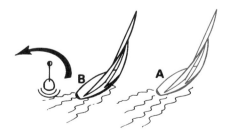

**18.2(c)** *ISAF Case 29. Establishing an overlap at a continuing obstruction.* W and L were running overlapped on the same gybe towards the finish, almost two lengths apart. M overtook and sailed between, establishing overlaps on both boats. There was no contact but W protested that M was not entitled to room because L was an obstruction to M and W, and M was clear astern when W came within two lengths of L. However, Rule 18.5 makes an exception to Rule 18.2(c) which states that M can establish an inside overlap on W provided there is room at that time to pass between W and L. Protest dismissed.

**18.2(c)** *ISAF Case 62.* A rounded ahead of B and sailed outside the two length zone. B rounded and because of the current and B's spinnaker blanketing A, A drifted towards B while B was still in the two-lengths zone. B was still obligated to keep clear of A under Rule 18.2(c) until both had completed their roundings.

**18.2(c)** *ISAF Case 63.* At a mark, when room is made available to a boat that has no right to it, she may, at her own risk, take advantage of the room so given.

**18.2(c)** *ISAF Case 81.* When two boats on the same tack are about to round a mark, Rule 18 applies even if they are on a beat. When one boat enters the two-boat-length circle clear ahead, Rule 18.2(c) applies. When the boat clear ahead then tacks, Rule 18.2(c) ceases to apply and she becomes subject to Rule 13 after passing head to wind and Rule 10 applies after she has reached close-hauled course.

**18.3** *ISAF Case 95.* Two boats are approaching a windward mark on port tack overlapped; W to windward just inside the zone, L one and a half lengths to leeward. L tacks for the layline without infringing Rules 13 or 15. W then tacks on top of L and luffs. L bears away to avoid W's transom and touches the mark. W is disqualified under Rule 18.3. Rule 18 did not apply before L's tack as he was not about to round. After her tack, Rule 18 still does not apply since they are now on opposite tacks. When W then tacks inside the zone she becomes subject to Rule 18.3.

**18.3(b)** *ISAF Case 93.* W completed a tack inside the two-length zone directly ahead of L but with room for L to pass between W and the mark. L bore away, established an inside overlap and then luffed and touched W. Had L not luffed W would have kept clear. L was disqualified under Rule 16. When one of two boats on opposite tacks completes a tack inside the zone, Rule 18.3 applies and therefore Rule 15 does not. However the leeward boat is still subject to Rule 16.

**18.4**     *ISAF Case 75.* Until an inside starboard-tack boat reaches the point in rounding a mark where her proper course is to gybe, an outside port-tack boat must keep clear under Rules 10 and 18.2(a). There is no conflict between Rules 10 and 18. Both apply and provide rights for the inside boat. The only limitation for the inside boat is not to pass farther from the mark than needed to sail her proper course as required by Rule 18.4.

**18.5**     *ISAF Case 16.* Boats overtaking overlapping boats clear ahead and attempting to sail between. L is an obstruction to W and M. Because the obstruction is moving in the same direction and with similar speed, it is a continuing obstruction. If the boats clear ahead are close together as here Rule 18.5 applies, in which case the boat clear astern is prohibited from making overlap on W and must keep clear.

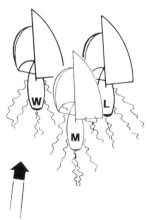

**18.5**     *ISAF Case 33.* Two overlapping boats were close-hauled. Both tacked and were still overlapped more than two lengths from a continuing obstruction. The new inside boat was entitled to invoke Rule 18.2(a) to pass the obstruction, the outer end of a breakwater.

**19.1**     *ISAF Case 35. The amount of room required when tacking at an obstruction.* After a reply of 'You Tack' to L's hail on approaching an obstruction, L tacked and was able to avoid W by three feet. L demonstrated by her actions that she had room under the prevailing conditions to tack and clear W.

**19.1**   *ISAF Case 54.* Two boats approaching the shore on starboard tack. The leeward boat is a length ahead and a length-and-a-half to leeward. The leeward boat hails but is not heard. W does not respond but L tacks, tries to bear away underneath the stern of W but hits her several feet forward of the transom. On this instance it seems that the hail was not adequate and a second louder hail should have been made. L was disqualified under Rules 10 and 14. However normally the hailing boat's judgment of her own safety is conclusive.

**19.1(a)**   *ISAF Case 3. Room to tack at an obstruction.* W and L, close-hauled and overlapped on port tack, were approached by S, close-hauled on starboard tack. S hailed for water; L hailed W to avoid S but obtained no response to three hails. S bore away to avoid a collision with L. W retired and S protested L who was disqualified under Rule 10. The Appeal Committee ruled that L did enough to satisfy her obligations. She was entitled to expect W to respond. She was not obliged to bear away astern of S or to anticipate W's failure to comply with Rule 19.1(a). So L was exonerated under Rule 64.1(a)

# PART 3 – CONDUCT OF A RACE

25     *ISAF Case 31. Race signals at the start.* Under these rules the timing of starting signals is governed by the visual signal. There must also be a sound signal but it need not be made at the same moment. A boat is under an obligation to start correctly, but if she is unaware that she started incorrectly and the signals have been incorrect she may be granted redress.

28.1     *ISAF Case 90.* A and B started correctly but because of wind and current they drifted backwards, A outside the port end start mark and B back over the line. When the wind came back from a new direction they both passed outside the starboard end of the line and up the course. When their 'strings' are drawn taut A's will pass between the starting marks even if it makes an extra turn round the whole starting line, but B's string will not pass through the starting line. A complies with Rule 28 but B does not.

28.2     *ISAF Case 58. Limit mark on the finishing line.* The inner limit mark was well on the post-finish side of the line. P crossed the line ahead of S, but well shorewards of the inner limit mark. Subsequently she passed the inner limit mark, leaving it to port. S, at the other end of the line, crossed the finishing line and left the outer limit mark to starboard. S requested redress saying that the Race Officer had finished P before she had rounded the inner limit mark and therefore before she had completed the course. The Protest Committee and later the Appeal Committee refused the request for redress. A buoy or other object on the post-finish side of the line is not a mark.

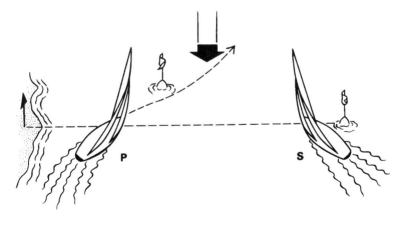

**29.2 + Race Signals**

*ISAF Case 71.* Hailing sail numbers is not the sound signal required by Rule 29.2 when flag X is displayed. Boats failing to start correctly because they did not hear the hail may be granted redress.

**29.2** *ISAF Case 79.* Several boats were slightly over the middle of the line at their starting signal. The Race Committee did not signal 'individual recall' by flag X and sound signal until 40 seconds after the start. When a boat has no reason to know she is early and the 'individual recall' is not signalled promptly, this is an error that entitles her to redress.

**30.3** *ISAF Case 96.* When, after a general recall, a boat learns from seeing her sail number displayed that she has been disqualified by the Race Committee and believes the Race Committee has made a mistake, her only option is not to start, and then to seek redress. When a boat breaks Rule 30.3 she is not entitled to exoneration because of a procedural error by the Race Committee that is unrelated to her infringement.

**31.3** *ISAF Case 28. Wrongfully compelled to touch a mark – abandoning after start.* A boat runs over a starting mark which sinks and re-surfaces, touching another boat on its pre-start side. Thus the second boat not only touched the mark but failed to start correctly since she passed the mark on the incorrect side. She has to return and re-start correctly to exonerate herself but she is not penalised for touching the mark. Abandonment is not an option open to the Committee in this case. Rule 32(d) abandoning after the start applies only to a mark that has shifted so that it is nowhere near its designated position.

**31.3(b)** *ISAF Case 56. Touching a mark.* A and B were involved in a collision and B hit the finishing mark. A protested but B neither protested nor exonerated herself. A was disqualified for not giving room but B was also disqualified for not protesting or taking a penalty as required by Rule 31.3(b). It is not enough that A protested over the same incident.

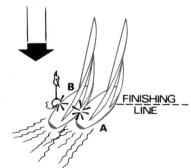

**32** *ISAF Case 37. Shortening or abandoning after the start.* Each race in a regatta is a separate race. In a multi-class regatta, abandonment may be suitable for some classes, but not for all.

# PART 4 – OTHER REQUIREMENTS WHEN RACING

**42.1** *ISAF Case 5. Propulsion.* Recovering an anchor rapidly may be propulsion contrary to Rule 42.1.

**42.1** *ISAF Case 8. Propulsion.* While reaching at good speed, a boat does not break Rule 42 when her helmsman, anticipating and taking advantage of following waves generated by a passing vessel, makes substantial helm movements timed to the passage of each wave. This is not sculling but using the natural action of water on the hull.

**42.1** *ISAF Case 69. Propulsion.* Momentum of a boat after the preparatory signal that is the result of being propelled by her engine before the signal does not break Rule 42.1.

**43.1(a)** *ISAF Case 89.* Wearing a drinking container on your person is not a necessity except on a sailboard. It is therefore considered to be for the purpose of increasing the competitor's weight and infringes Rule 43.

**46** *ISAF Case 40. Person in charge.* Unless specifically stated in the Class Rules, Notice of Race or prescribed in the Sailing Instructions, the owner or person in charge of a boat is free to decide who steers her in a race, provided Rule 46 is not broken.

**49.2** *ISAF Case 83.* Repeated sail-trimming with the torso outside the lifelines is not permitted.

**50.3(a)** *ISAF Case 4. Definition of an outrigger.* An outrigger is defined as a 'fitting', the crew's hand is not a 'fitting' and can therefore be used to hold a sheet outboard.

**50.3** *ISAF Case 97.* A spinnaker guy is not a sheet, so a jockey pole attached to a spinnaker guy is not an outrigger for a sheet.

# PART 5 – PROTESTS, HEARINGS, MISCONDUCT AND APPEALS

## Section A – Protests

**60**   ***ISAF Case 39.*** After a series several boats protested A for breaking a class rule limiting the crew to two. The protests were refused because none of the protesting boats had displayed protest flags. This decision was appealed on the grounds that the Race Committee ought, on its own initiative, to have protested A in all the races. Appeal dismissed. A Race Committee is under no obligation to protest a boat.

**60**   ***ISAF Case 80.*** When A crossed the finishing line she was scored DNF because the Race Committee believed she had failed to sail the course correctly. A requested redress claiming she had finished according to the definition. Redress was denied but A appealed and was reinstated. Without a hearing, a boat may not be penalised for failing to sail the course. The Race Committee should have protested A. A protest hearing and decision must be limited to a particular incident that has been described in the protest so A could not be penalised for failing to sail the course during the redress hearing. The Race Committee should have protested A for failing to sail the course.

**60.1**   ***ISAF Case 1.*** *Right to protest.* A boat which breaks a rule during a race and continues, can subsequently protest over a later incident even though she is disqualified after the race for the first incident.

**60.1**   ***ISAF Case 68.*** *Right to protest – sportsmanship.* The principles of sportsmanship obligate a boat to take a penalty or retire when she realises that she has broken a rule, but if she continues to race she retains her rights under Part 2 and her right to protest or request redress. The failure of a Race Committee to discover that a rating certificate is invalid does not entitle another boat to redress.

**61.1**   ***ISAF Case 42.*** If an incident occurs in the racing area, a boat intending to protest must hail 'protest' and display a red flag at the first reasonable opportunity, even if the protesting boat is not directly involved in the incident. Failure of her hail to be heard does not invalidate the protest. A protestee not knowing she was being protested is not, by itself, grounds for not hearing the case. Evidence of rule infringement by a boat that is not a party to the protest at the hearing of a valid protest permits a Protest Committee to proceed against that boat.

**61.1(a)** *ISAF Case 72.* An object used as a flag must visually communicate the message 'I intend to protest' with little or no possibility of causing confusion on the part of the other competitors. A flag must be seen primarily to be a flag.

**61.2(c)** *ISAF Case 22.* A Protest Committee's refusal of a protest cannot be justified by the fact that the rule alleged to have been infringed and cited in the protest was incorrect.

**62** *ISAF Case 44. Redress.* A boat may request redress under the provisions of Rule 62, but only on the grounds that, through no fault of her own, an improper act or omission of the Race Committee made her finishing position significantly worse. The rules do not permit a Race Committee to be protested or penalised.

## Section B – Hearings and Decisions

**63.2** *ISAF Case 48.* A helmsman appealed a decision on the grounds that he was aware that a hearing was being held only when he was told to attend it. He had to read the protest while the hearing was in progress, and was not given time to prepare. The protest had been lodged in time, the time of the hearing had been posted correctly and the protest had been available for reading for more than an hour. Part 5 aims to protect a boat from miscarriage of justice, not to provide loopholes for protestees. A protestee has a duty to protect himself by acting reasonably before a hearing.

**64.1** *ISAF Case 10.* P on port did not keep clear and caused M on starboard to tack and make contact with S. P retired but M was disqualified. M appealed successfully. When two boats make contact, both may be exonerated when the situation was caused by a third boat that infringed a rule.

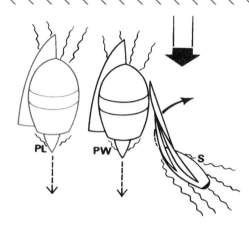

**64.1**    *ISAF Case 49.* Two boats, PL and PW, were broad reaching in a lot of wind on port tack. They were on a collision course with boat S which was beating to windward on starboard tack. S was an obstruction to PW under Rule 18.2(a) who required room from PL to avoid a collision. There was contact of rigging between S and PW. S protested PW and PW protested PL. The protests were heard separately. PW was disqualified under Rule 10 and PL under Rule 18.2(a). PW appealed and was reinstated. Rule 10 required the port tack boat to keep clear but PW was unable to, because PL did not give sufficient room. No hail was required by PW as both port gybe boats were aware of boat S. When protests arise from the same, or closely connected incidents, it is advisable to hear them together in the presence of all the boats involved

## Section C – Gross Misconduct

**69.1**    *ISAF Case 34. Action by a Protest Committee and Rule 2, Fair Sailing.* Deliberately starting prematurely and harassing another boat in order to win a series constitutes gross infringement of the rules and sportsmanship, and could be the basis for action by the Protest Committee under Rule 69.1. Exclusion from the entire series would have been well within the spirit of the Racing Rules.

# Section D – Appeals

70    *ISAF Case 55. Right of appeal.* A 'protested' the Race Committee because of inadequate rescue facilities in contravention of the club's deeds. The Race Committee abandoned the completed race. B's appeal was denied. A boat has no right of appeal from a redress decision when she is not involved in the hearing. When she believes that her finishing position has been made worse by the decision she must herself request redress. She may then appeal the decision of that hearing.

71.4   *ISAF Case 61. Appeal decisions.* When the decision of a Protest Committee is reversed upon appeal, the final standings and the awards must be adjusted accordingly.

# PART 6 – ENTRY AND QUALIFICATION

**78.3**   *ISAF Case 57. Compliance with class rules.* Two IOR-rated boats sailed in a summer-long series. A was later found to have sailed the series with an incorrect rating certificate. B requested redress. It was subsequently found by the National Rating Authority that there was an error in the rating certificate dating from the first hull measurement some years back. The Protest Committee found that the owner of boat A was not responsible for the error and that he had not infringed Rule 78.1. The Protest Committee decided that the Race Committee was not responsible for the error and therefore boat B was not entitled to redress. An in-date, duly authenticated certificate, presented in good faith, by an owner who has complied with the requirements of Rule 78.1, cannot be retrospectively invalidated after a race or series is completed.

# PART 7 – RACE ORGANIZATION

**86.1c**   *ISAF Case 85.* A class tried to delete Rule 61.1 which requires flying of protest flags. Rule 61 is not listed in Rule 86.1c among rules that the class rules can change. Class rules may not alter a racing rule unless the alteration is permitted by the racing rule itself.

**88.2c**   *ISAF Case 32. Change in sailing instructions and oral briefing.* The Sailing Instructions cannot require a competitor to attend an oral briefing. He is entitled to expect all necessary information to be contained in the written Sailing Instructions, possibly with amendments made in accordance with Rule 86.2.

**85**   *ISAF Case 66. Protest Committee.* A Race Committee has no jurisdiction over a Jury and may not alter, or refuse to implement, the decision of a Jury or independent Protest Committee, including a decision based on a report from an authority qualified to resolve questions of measurement.

# RACE SIGNALS

The meanings of visual and sound signals are stated below. For the colour of flags and sound signals see back cover. When a visual signal is displayed over a class flag, the signal applies only to that class.

**AP**   Races not started are *postponed.* The warning signal will be made 1 minute after removal unless at that time the race is postponed again or abandoned.

**AP over a numeral pennant 1–6:** *Postponement* of 1–6 hours from the scheduled starting time.

**AP over H:** Races not started are *postponed.* Further signals ashore.

**AP over A:**  Races not started are *postponed.* No more racing today.

**C**    The position of the next *mark* has been changed.

**I**     Rule 30.1 is in effect.

**L**    Ashore: A notice to competitors has been posted.
Afloat: Come within hail or follow this boat.

**M**   The object displaying this signal replaces a missing *mark.*

**N**    All races that have started are *abandoned.* Return to the starting area. The warning signal will be made 1 minute after removal unless at that time the race is abandoned again or postponed.

**N over H:** All races are *abandoned.* Further signals ashore.

**N over A:** All races are *abandoned.* No more racing today.

**P**    Preparatory signal.

**S**    No later than the warning signal: Sail the short course.
At a rounding or finishing *mark: Finish* between the nearby *mark* and the staff displaying this flag.

**X**    Individual recall.

**Y**    Wear personal buoyancy.

**Z**    Rule 30.2 is in effect.

**First substitute:** General recall. The warning signal will be made 1 minute after removal.

**Black flag:** Rule 30.3 is in effect.

**Blue flag or shape:** This Race Committee boat is in position at the finishing line.

Published by Adlard Coles Nautical 2001
an imprint of A & C Black (Publishers) Ltd
35 Bedford Row, London WC1R 4JH
www.adlardcoles.co.uk

ISBN 0-7136-5858-4

First published in Great Britain by
Creagh-Osborne & Partners Ltd December 1965
Reprinted May 1966, February 1967
Second edition January 1969
Reprinted June 1969, August 1971
Third edition April 1973
Reprinted July 1973, September 1974
Fourth edition February 1977
Fifth edition February 1981
Sixth edition edition published by Adlard Coles June 1985
Reprinted September 1985
Seventh edition 1989
Eighth edition published by Adlard Coles Nautical 1993
Ninth edition 1997
Tenth edition 2001

A CIP catalogue record for this book is available from the British Library.

Design and computer page make up by Penny Mills
Typeset in 8.5/10pt Photina
Printed and bound in Great Britain by Haynes Publishing, Sparkford,
Somerset